KU-346-359

# the buddha book

# the buddha book

GILL FARRER-HALLS

First published in Great Britain in 2003
by Godsfield Press,
a division of Octopus Publishing Group Ltd
2–4 Heron Quays, London E14 4JP.

This edition published in 2005



Printed and bound in China

ISBN 1-84181-294-3
EAN 9781841812946

10 9 8 7 6 5 4 3 2 1

# contents


| | |
|---|---|
| introduction | 6 |
| buddhist principles | 8 |
| buddhist meditation | 40 |
| buddhist traditions | 68 |
| devotional buddhism | 102 |
| index | 126 |
| acknowledgments | 128 |

# introduction

*Suffering I teach, and the way out of suffering . . .*

THE BUDDHA

The first time I saw a statue of the Buddha it made a strong impression. The attribute that struck me most powerfully was the quality of benign peace that seemed to radiate from the finely sculpted features. I knew little about Buddhism at the time, but seeing the statue piqued my curiosity. When I traveled to India some years later, I was determined to find out what lay behind the extraordinary and peaceful expression of the Buddha.

I discovered that the Buddha was an ordinary human being, like you and me. After much diligent, dedicated meditation and other spiritual practices, he finally became enlightened. His enlightenment was not a mystical, transcendental experience bestowed upon him by some superior god. Rather, it was an awakening to his own true nature and the liberation from suffering that naturally followed. The essence of what the Buddha taught is that suffering permeates our lives but that there is an end to suffering.

The religion that evolved after his death is obviously based on what the Buddha taught, but it has developed in diverse ways. The Buddha's teachings spread to different countries and were assimilated into various cultures, alongside each culture's existing indigenous religious beliefs and practices.

Buddhist scholars, meditators, mystics, and practitioners have been inspired over the centuries to provide different interpretations, which has also affected the development of Buddhism.

Despite the differences in Buddhist traditions, at the heart of each lies the Buddha's message of the potential of awakening for us all. We can perceive the rich diversity of traditions as a skillful legacy, whereby each person can follow the approach that is best suited to their character and disposition. Buddhism continues to evolve as it encounters modern Western cultures, and remains a vibrant spiritual tradition today.

This book is a simple introduction to Buddha's timeless teachings, which are as relevant today as they have always been. To begin, the basic principles of Buddhism are described in the context of the unique features of the different traditions. Next, there is an explanation of meditation and how it can be of benefit to you, together with instructions on how to meditate. Then the different Buddhist traditions are outlined. Finally, the devotional aspect of Buddhism is introduced and instructions are given on how to use a Buddha statue, incense, and prayer beads.

*The way of the Buddha is to know yourself, to know yourself is to forget yourself, to forget yourself is to be enlightened by all things.*

DOGEN

# buddhist principles

# why buddhism?

*The* Dharma *(the teachings of the Buddha) is not something to believe in, but something to do.*

STEPHEN BATCHELOR

For the newcomer to Buddhism, questions naturally arise, such as "What distinguishes Buddhism from other religions?" and "What can Buddhism offer that is unique?" As the quotation above suggests, Buddhism is a way of life rather than simply a set of beliefs. This way of life was offered by the Buddha as a path that leads practitioners away from suffering and toward happiness. This is something everyone must discover for themselves through experience; you cannot simply adopt a set of beliefs and expect to find instant happiness.

The emphasis on taking personal responsibility for your own welfare is perhaps the most distinguishing feature of Buddhism. The Buddha pointed to craving (or desire) as the root cause of suffering, and taught that suffering decreases only by abandoning desire. Desire is very difficult to relinquish because it is a fundamental instinct, and so Buddhism offers a multitude of logical arguments, meditations, and philosophies to challenge the insidious presence of desire. The Buddha was a living example of someone who managed to relinquish all desire; his example shows that, although this is an extraordinarily difficult task, it is possible.

Buddhism is culturally embedded in the East, but the essence of Buddhism does not lie in the foreign cultural trappings of Asia. Some Westerners are attracted by colorful monastic robes, strange gods, and exotic rituals. But these superficial cultural expressions are much less significant than the central message that Buddha taught, which lies beneath the surface of appearances.

Buddhism—like many religions—has the usual trappings of institutions, priests, and regulations. Many Westerners have moved away from organized religion because the modern way of life can leave little time or appetite for such religious paraphernalia. The relentless drive to consumerism and greed for materialistic gratification have more power over people's lives these days. Buddhism helps us overcome materialism by revealing impermanence, not only of the things we crave, but also of our own lives.

Many people recognize a lack of spirituality in their lives and are concerned about the meaning of birth and death, and of life in between. Buddhism still offers a path of inquiry into our experience of life, as well as methods to help us wake up to the truth of enlightenment that the Buddha Shakyamuni (the historical Buddha) discovered in his own lifetime many years ago.

# how buddhism helps us find stress relief and contentment

*There is no way to happiness; happiness is the way.*

BUDDHA SHAKYAMUNI

The principles of Buddhism are simple to grasp, but it takes time and experience to learn how to practice them well. However, Buddhism is also a profound philosophy that has been developed and refined over the centuries by leading Buddhist masters throughout Asia. Some of these great sages spent many years living in remote caves practicing meditation; others were great teachers who helped their students discover the benefits of Buddhism. Yet all remained convinced of the main tenet of Buddhism because they had discovered it in their own lives. The foremost reason to

follow the Buddha's path is that it ultimately leads to happiness and the elimination of suffering.

Buddhism has two ways to help us discover the elusive, stress free, contented life we all long for. The first is to listen to or read about the Buddha's teachings, and to try to understand them by reflecting deeply on them during meditation. Secondly, when we are convinced that what the Buddha taught will improve our lives, we try to imbue each moment with mindful awareness of living our lives according to the Buddhist teachings.

To some extent, the two kinds of happiness that we experience—physical comfort and mental peace—are interrelated. Mental peace is the more important of the two. If our mind is contented and peaceful, we can be more accepting of our physical problems, such as pain. If the mind is stressed and miserable, we will never be truly happy, even if our body is pain free or we live in luxury with many material possessions. So training the mind with meditation helps reduce stress and cultivates peace and contentment, which lead to a happy life.

# the buddha's life story

*Despite the many developments through which the religious tradition that bears his name has gone, the historical Buddha remains fundamental.*

JOHN SNELLING

The man who was to become the Buddha was born an Indian prince called Siddhartha Gautama around 2,500 years ago. A wise old soothsayer called Asita was asked to bless the child. During the blessing Asita predicted that the child would grow up to be either a great king like his father or a renowned religious teacher. King Shuddhodana, eager for his son to succeed him, decided to keep Siddhartha confined within the palace grounds and kept from anything unpleasant. The father hoped the son would not wish to explore life outside if he was surrounded by luxury.

The prince grew up to be an accomplished young man, got married, and had a son. But even with every wish fulfilled, Siddhartha remained curious about life outside the palace. Finally his father permitted him to visit the local town. During his excursion, Siddhartha was deeply affected by the sight of an old person, a sick person, and a corpse. Having realized that all beings, including himself, would experience the sufferings of old age, sickness, and death, he fled the palace and embarked upon the spiritual life. Siddhartha studied with the great spiritual teachers of the day, but although he became an accomplished meditator he still faced the dilemmas of life and death. After an ascetic period of fasting, he was offered a bowl of milk and rice, which he accepted. As the food strengthened his body, he realized that extreme asceticism was no more the answer than his earlier life of indulgence. So he resolved to sit under a tree in meditation until he reached awakening. As the eighth day dawned and he saw the morning star, he finally became an enlightened one—the Buddha Shakyamuni.

The Buddha spent the rest of his life teaching and helping others to find awakening from his spontaneous compassionate response to their suffering. He created a set of guidelines based on meditation, ethics, and wisdom for his disciples to follow in their search for liberation from suffering. Many people were ordained as mendicant monks and nuns and joined him in the homeless life, meditating in the forest and wandering from town to town. When he passed away, his teachings were carried on by his followers and developed into what we now know as Buddhism.

# the relevance of buddha's life

*Prince Siddhartha's dilemma still faces us today.*

STEPHEN BATCHELOR

Although the Buddha was happy to help people awaken, he was unconcerned with creating a religion or appointing a successor. This was not because the Buddha did not care about helping the generations of people who would live after his lifetime. To the contrary, his life and teachings point directly to his wish to be of benefit to all others. But by not creating a religious hierarchy, the Buddha left the door of opportunity open for everyone, from whatever culture or time, to follow his teachings for themselves in their quest to alleviate suffering.

One human life is much like another once the veneer of culture and wealth—or lack of it—has been stripped away. Prince Siddhartha saw this the moment he left the palace for the first time. He realized that the suffering from which he had been shielded—illness, old age, and death—could, and would, happen to him as well as to all other beings. Although we may not have experienced early years of confined luxury like Prince Siddhartha, we do share the prison of illusion that contemporary society encourages.

The realities of suffering and sickness, old age and death, are obscured by the modern obsession with acquiring wealth, sensual gratification, and social status. In this way, the experience of dissatisfaction that permeates our lives

today bears a resemblance to the Buddha's dissatisfaction before he awakened. The story of the Buddha's life clearly reveals that the root of dissatisfaction does not lie in external circumstances of privilege or its lack. Dissatisfaction exists while we remain at the mercy of desire and we can never find the calm peace of the awakened state until we let go of our craving. But the possibility of liberation is there, demonstrated by Buddha's own awakening, and remains a potential for us all. Among Buddha's last words is his advice: "Strive on with awareness." We can all awaken—but it takes great mindfulness and effort.

# the four noble truths

*If my desires are unable to be fulfilled even by everything upon this earth, what else will be able to satisfy them?*

SHANTIDEVA

The Buddha's first teaching is known as the Four Noble Truths. These are: **1. Recognizing the existence of suffering; 2. Understanding the causes of suffering; 3. Believing in the cessation of the causes of suffering; 4. Following the path that leads to the cessation of the causes of suffering.** This is the essence of Buddhism.

The First Noble Truth refers to the fact that suffering—ranging from mild dissatisfaction to absolute misery—permeates our existence. Yet we sometimes don't even realize that we are suffering. The first thing to do is to acknowledge that there is suffering in life and that we continually experience it. Although we do experience happiness, if you examine the times you have been happy you will discover only fleeting moments that disappeared, bringing suffering in their wake.

Dissatisfaction is inherent in our nature because—as the Buddha pointed out—we are born, get sick, grow old, and eventually die. Though this might seem a rather negative view at first, after reflection it appears a realistic assessment of existence. This makes us curious about what causes suffering, so we turn to the Second Noble Truth.

The Second Noble Truth is that suffering has a cause. The primary cause of suffering is desire. You might perhaps think that external circumstances cause suffering. But although life's difficulties certainly can aggravate suffering, they are not the direct cause. Desires arise continually and we crave their fulfilment. But even when we are lucky and get our heart's desire, look what happens. We start to want something else almost immediately. The precious object, lover, or experience no longer gives full satisfaction. Many of our desires remain unfulfilled and we don't like what we have instead, so desire itself is clearly the main problem, together with anger, pride, ignorance, doubt, and wrong views.

The Third Noble Truth is the cessation of suffering and its causes, which we know is possible because the Buddha attained enlightenment. This is described as *nirvana*, a Sanskrit word that means "the cessation of suffering." The awakened, enlightened state of liberation from suffering is impossible to describe adequately; it is something that has to be experienced. Nonetheless, it is clear that enlightenment is the extinguishing of desire and suffering. Suffering and the delusions that cause suffering need not be permanent and their cycle can be broken—which brings us to the Fourth Noble Truth.

The Fourth Noble Truth is that Buddhism provides a set of guidelines for living well in a way that will eventually bring freedom from being driven by desire and, ultimately, the end of suffering. Different schools of Buddhism describe this path in different ways, but the essence is encapsulated in the Noble Eightfold Path, described at the end of this chapter, in which the Buddha offers eight practical ways to lessen desire.

# the three jewels

*The Three Jewels are the Buddha, the Dharma, and the Sangha. It is by committing one's life to these three principles that one is considered a Buddhist.*

STEPHEN BATCHELOR

The Three Jewels are considered to be one of the most important foundations of Buddhism, and taking refuge in the Three Jewels is a fundamental basis of Buddhist practice. The First Jewel is the Buddha, who is the personification of enlightened wisdom and compassion. We take refuge in the Buddha because he has gone beyond suffering, and can guide us toward our own awakening. Taking refuge in the Buddha allows us to rely on his enlightened qualities as we nurture our own buddha nature—the seeds of enlightenment within ourselves.

The Dharma refers to the Buddha's teachings, which contain all knowledge and wisdom required to follow the Buddhist path until the goal of awakening is reached. Some schools of Buddhism hold personal nirvana as the ultimate goal, while others strive for enlightenment for all beings. The Sanskrit word *Dharma* means "to hold," which in this context refers to holding or protecting us from ignorance. Taking refuge in the Dharma helps us work toward freedom from suffering. We train our minds and cultivate wisdom by studying and following the Buddha's teachings.

The Sangha refers to the spiritual community of Buddhists. The term *Sangha* is sometimes applied specifically to mean only the monastic community, but in the broader sense refers to our spiritual friends; those who share our Buddhist beliefs and who offer support and encouragement in following the Buddhist path. Taking refuge in the Sangha means we rely on our Buddhist teachers and friends who help us understand how to apply the Buddha's teachings in our lives. When we encounter problems, our spiritual friends can help us resolve them skillfully.

Taking refuge in the Three Jewels involves a brief but formal ceremony with a Buddhist monastic teacher, or guru, which people undertake when they feel ready to embark on the Buddhist path. Each of the Buddhist traditions has a prayer of refuge that is recited daily as part of a personal Buddhist practice or meditation session. The refuge prayer is often also recited together with other participants during formal Buddhist ceremonies. The frequency of repetition means that one's commitment to the Buddhist path is continuously renewed. In this way the Buddha, Dharma, and Sangha remain a constant source of inspiration and spiritual strength during your daily life.

# the three poisons

*We can never be at peace while desire is nagging at us.*

JOHN SNELLING

The Buddhist picture of the Wheel of Life symbolically represents how we remain trapped in negative behavior patterns that cause repeated suffering. At the center of the Wheel of Life three animals are depicted, which symbolize the Three Poisons. Each poisonous behavioral trait causes—and is reinforced by—the other two. The three animals are painted head to tail and are eating each other, which is a potent symbol of endless cycles of suffering.

The pig represents ignorance, blindness, and delusion. This refers to our mistaken ideas of how the world and everything in it exists. We tend to believe that things exist by themselves, independent of their various components and their surrounding circumstances and conditions. This view causes us to believe that some of these things are capable of providing us with lasting satisfaction. Furthermore, we believe ourselves to exist in this independent fashion too.

This fundamental ignorance causes desire to arise, which is symbolized by the rooster. Because we believe objects and sensations can bring enduring happiness, desire, craving, and lust continuously arise. This causes only suffering because either our desires are thwarted and we remain in a state of unfulfilled longing, or we get what we want but shortly after we crave something else.

Unsatisfied desire causes hostility to arise, which is symbolized by the snake. Because of our ignorant view that we exist independently of others, we believe that it is most important to fulfill our own desires even at the expense of others. So when we see other people who have the objects we crave, this causes us to feel jealous anger or envious hatred.

Anger and hatred cloud our thinking, so when we are under the malevolent force of these negative emotions we are unable to inquire into our mistaken perception of the world, which keeps us in ignorance. Outside of the Wheel of Life the Buddha stands free from the cycle of suffering perpetrated by the Three Poisons. He symbolizes the awakened state of liberation from suffering. Taking refuge in the Three Jewels helps us liberate ourselves from the Three Poisons.

# love and compassion

*There are many different philosophies, but what is of basic importance is compassion, love for others . . .*

H. H. THE DALAI LAMA

Love is the wish for all beings to be happy. Usually we are selective in who we love, reserving these feelings for friends and family. However, when love is limited and conditional it tends to become tainted with attachment and expectation. We feel that if we love someone, then they should love us in return. Also, love can quickly turn to hate if the loved person decides that he or she no longer wants to be friends with us. This is attachment, not love.

Because love is a bottomless lake we don't need to be stingy with it. Love will not run out if we extend it, so we can afford to be generous. What stops us from loving everyone? It is because we discriminate between people. We are attracted to some, repelled by others, and indifferent to many. Yet these partisan feelings are unreliable since they change. Your dear friend was once unknown; your hated ex-lover was once your closest friend. Abandoning discrimination helps us realize it is possible to want all others to be happy, which is the true expression of love.

Compassion is the heartfelt wish for all beings to be free from suffering. In the same way that we ourselves want to be happy and free from suffering, so do all other beings. Love and compassion for others is essential for our own happiness because we can never be truly happy and free from suffering while those around us suffer unhappiness. However, we don't need to feel sad to be compassionate toward others. Being overly emotional is sentimentality rather than true compassion.

Developing a compassionate attitude toward others is more realistic than believing we can relieve all their suffering. This doesn't mean you shouldn't try to help when you can, but it is important not to feel despondent when you can't. Understanding how suffering occurs, knowing what you can do to help when you are able to, and not worrying when you can't—these things are true compassion.

For love and compassion to flourish, the Buddhist teachings encourage us to equate ourselves with others. This means seeing the needs and wishes of others as equally important—if not more so—than our own. Relinquishing our self-centered desires and seeking to be of benefit to others helps us find happiness.

# generosity and morality

*Wealth is a result of generosity,*
*whereas poverty is a result of avarice.*

GESHE RABTEN

The Sanskrit word for generosity is *dana*, which means "giving" or "charity." More specifically we can say that dana is the spirit of generosity combined with acts of giving. The Buddhist teachings describe three types of generosity: giving material assistance to those in need; giving protection to those in fear or danger; and giving Buddhist teachings when requested.

All those in need are worthy of assistance, and to help develop the mind of generosity it is beneficial not to discriminate between those we want to help and those we don't care about. It is important to be realistic about how much you can afford to give—neither too much nor too little. If you cannot afford to give much, even thinking about those in need with kindness helps develop generosity.

The modern world offers many opportunities to give assistance to those in fear and danger. Helping people who have been robbed or attacked, and helping refugees who are fearful for their lives are examples of acts of generosity. Generosity includes helping animals in danger. Giving Buddhist teachings may seem ambitious when you are just learning about Buddhism, but the essence of what Buddha taught is kindness and compassion. You can always mention these qualities if asked to say something about Buddhism.

For those who have committed themselves to Buddhism, morality, or moral discipline, means keeping vows and commitments. In a general Buddhist sense, for anyone who wishes to follow the Buddhist path, morality means both abandoning negative actions and cultivating good qualities. Buddhism lists ten nonvirtuous actions from which we should try to refrain: These are: telling lies, slandering others, mindlessly and maliciously gossiping about others, swearing and shouting angrily, killing, stealing, sexual misconduct, craving and attachment, wishing to harm others, and believing wrong views. It is unlikely that we can be perfectly moral when we first try, but being mindful of negative behavior helps us gradually to abandon it.

Adhering rigidly to a moral code without understanding why it is beneficial can lead to self-satisfied piety. The Buddha taught that the positive effects of morality and moral discipline are peace and clarity of mind. When we are free of negative emotions, wisdom and compassion naturally arise. We can see from our own experience that when we do something we know is wrong our mind remains agitated and troubled, but when we are kind to others we feel happy to have helped them.

# patience and joyful effort

*There is no evil like hatred, and no fortitude like patience.*

SHANTIDEVA

It is natural to feel impatient when our plans go awry or when we experience suffering. But such impatience often leads to negative reactions, such as anger, which cause suffering for ourselves and others. Impatience is a manifestation of the ego that remains blind to the reality of other factors and the wishes of other people. It is focused only on the fulfillment of its own desires here and now. Therefore, patience requires insight into the nature of reality. We need to accept that things don't always go our way and realize that our urgent desire for something now may be forgotten in a few days' time.

Buddhism recommends that we practice patience in the face of suffering—to remain calm and retain our precious peace of mind even when we are attacked by others. In this way, we only have to deal with the external suffering. We do not cause further suffering to arise through our feelings of impatience. We cannot prevent problems from arising. That is simply the nature of life. But transforming how we react to them by practicing patience helps us lessen suffering and deal with the problems more effectively.

Joyful effort is the determination and resolve to accomplish what we have set out to do with enthusiasm. In daily life, we need determination to fulfill our obligations at work, to our friends, and at home. In Buddhism, joyful effort refers to maintaining our willingness to keep on meditating, cultivating positive attitudes, and relinquishing negative emotions and behavior—even when we feel discouraged and want to give up.

Whenever we feel inadequate or lazy, cultivating joyful effort helps us overcome this negative passivity. Reflecting upon and experiencing the many benefits of practicing Buddhism gives us motivation to continue, even when it seems difficult or when we encounter setbacks. Joyful effort is joyful; we feel inspired to follow the Buddha's teachings because we understand that it leads toward peace and happiness. If we try to accomplish something only because we feel we should and do not see the benefits, then we are much less likely to succeed.

# concentration and wisdom

*A single-pointed mind is the fully trained state of the meditative mind. It serves as the ground for cultivating wisdom . . .*

GESHE WANGCHEN

Pure concentration is referred to as single-pointed mind because all distractions and mental wanderings have been subdued. This allows the mind to focus without wavering on a single object. We develop this single-pointed concentration by practicing calm meditation, which is described in Chapter 2. Calm meditation is also called mindfulness meditation since it both calms the mind and improves awareness, which are both necessary to develop single-pointed concentration.

The ultimate purpose of developing concentration is to allow the mind to penetrate deeply into an object of meditation in order to realize its true nature. The object of meditation can be either a physical object such as a statue of the Buddha or a metaphysical object such as the nature of mind, or compassion. To develop concentration we need to prepare our minds with mindfulness meditation. We also need to establish good motivation and a suitably peaceful environment. Then we practice single-pointed concentration frequently and diligently, avoiding wandering thoughts and mental dullness, until we experience the benefits of an alert, clear, and stable mind.

Wisdom in the Buddhist sense does not mean just the acquisition of knowledge, but is a way of experientially understanding how phenomena, including yourself, actually exist. Wisdom arises through meditation when you observe your experience from moment to moment. As you see thoughts and emotions arise and pass, you develop an understanding of impermanence. This is reinforced through examining how objects exist and realizing that nothing is permanent.

Understanding impermanence helps lessen the view that things exist in a concrete fashion, independently of their parts, causes, and surrounding conditions. In this way wisdom realizes the lack of inherent existence, or emptiness, of phenomena. This doesn't mean things don't exist but merely that their existence depends on many factors. Wisdom arises through understanding and insight into your experience of yourself and the surrounding world. Wisdom then helps you understand and avoid the causes of suffering and cultivate behavior that leads toward happiness.

# impermanence and death

*Just like a dream experience, whatever things I enjoy will become a memory. Whatever has passed will not be seen again.*

SHANTIDEVA

To shield ourselves from the unpleasant facts of impermanence and death we create the illusion of permanence. This leads to the false belief that objects and people can make us happy. However, our treasured possessions deteriorate, break, or are lost. Our friends move on elsewhere, lose interest in our relationship with them, or die. Each of us knows that we too will die, yet we tend to assume we will live to be old. We persist in hiding from the reality of impermanence and death despite being surrounded with evidence to the contrary.

The Buddha once remarked that, just as the elephant's footprint is the biggest footprint of all the animals, so meditation on impermanence is the most powerful meditation. We can easily witness impermanence in the rotting apple, the broken vase, and the torn dress. In this way we verify impermanence from our own experience. We see people around us become wrinkled and grey because they are growing old. This is irrefutable evidence of impermanence. When we meditate on impermanence we strip away the illusion of constancy and wake up to the transitory nature of life.

The realization of impermanence is extremely poignant. It is a somber response to the brevity of existence that invites us to value what we have here and now because in a moment it could all be lost. In the same way, being aware of death paradoxically allows us to value life more and to live every moment meaningfully.

When we reflect on the fragility of life—the fact that our existence depends on the next breath, the next heartbeat—then we realize the value of following a spiritual path like Buddhism. It is certain we will die, and the time and manner of our death are uncertain. Material possessions, friends, and family are of no use at the time of death. Our wonderful experiences and great learning are gone forever.

The only thing of any use when we approach death is the calm mind that comes from meditating and following the path to awakening. So now is the time to listen to the Buddha's teachings and start living a mindful, spiritual life so we can face death with peace. In this way we can fully appreciate our precious human lives while we still have them.

# interdependence and lovingkindness

*All phenomena exist interdependently.*

GESHE RABTEN

In contrast to Christianity, Buddhist teachings have no concept of a Creator God. Buddhism also teaches that things are not self-created, nor do they exist independently of their causes and conditions. This leads logically to the philosophy of interdependence, or dependent origination, which posits that all phenomena exist in dependence on their causes, circumstances, attributes, and constituent parts.

The whole of life is, therefore, an intricate web of relationships in which everything depends on everything else. There is a beautiful image to describe this complex network, called Indra's Jeweled Net. At every junction of the

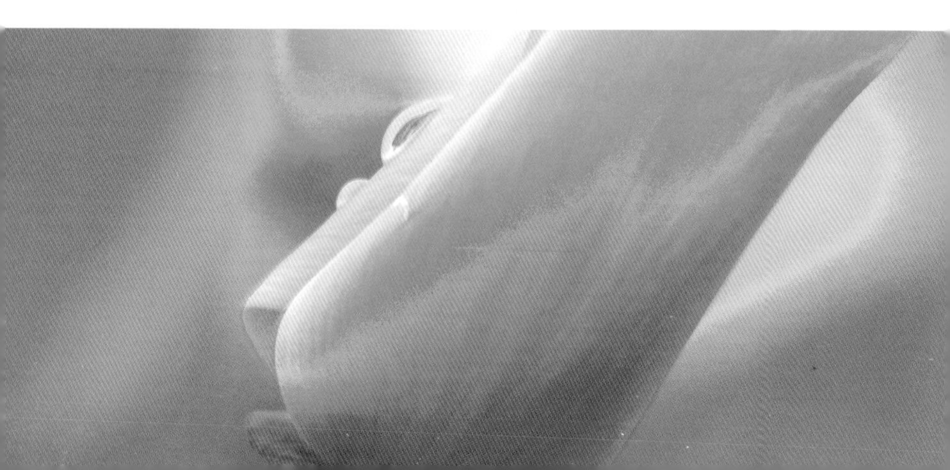

net lies a multifaceted jewel, and each single jewel is reflected in every other jewel. In this way, even one tiny change affects the whole. This means that everything we experience and all of our actions are influenced by other factors. In the same way, we influence everything around us.

Understanding interdependence helps you reduce your level of attachment to your self-interest and develop a sense of responsibility to others. You understand that you cannot find happiness if those around you are not also happy. Similarly, you learn to respect and care for your environment because you know you depend on it for your continued well-being and existence.

Once we see how life exists interdependently, it is a natural step to embrace the practice of lovingkindness, because discrimination between self and others is naturally lessened. Lovingkindness is the genuine feeling of concern for the happiness and well-being of others. We must also develop lovingkindness toward ourselves. Sometimes we believe that we don't deserve to be happy or we judge ourselves harshly. Loving and accepting ourselves is the first step toward developing lovingkindness toward others.

Lovingkindness is spaciousness of mind and openness of heart, a natural feeling of benevolence toward others that frees you from narrow-minded self-centeredness. This means that you regard all others without partiality and wish them happiness. You see all other human beings—and animals—as being just like yourself in their desire to find happiness and avoid suffering. Therefore, you naturally respond with thoughts of lovingkindness that wish for all beings to be well and happy.

# buddhism in action: the noble eightfold path

*The way to the cessation of all suffering, which is liberation or freedom, is the fourth noble truth, the noble eightfold path.*

AYYA KHEMA

The Noble Eightfold Path leads to the cessation of suffering and its causes. The eight points of the path are integral to the Three Higher Trainings in Buddhism of morality, meditation, and wisdom. These mutually supportive and inseparable practices are cultivated simultaneously, and their mutually enriching totality is greater than the individual parts. The best approach to the eight points is to understand each one as reinforcing the others.

**Right View** is the foundation of the Buddhist path. The first step is to learn that suffering permeates existence, but that there is a way out. Then we must try out if what Buddha taught leads to awakening. If we do not test his teachings in our own lives we are taking them on trust, which is no more than blind faith. Our views shape our perceptions and establish our values, creating a framework through which we interpret the world and the meaning of existence. Buddha taught that there were two distinct views. Wrong View leads toward actions that cause suffering. Right View guides us toward Right Action and ultimately toward liberation from suffering.

**Right Thought** is about developing good motivation. Right Thought helps us change our habitual self-centered thinking, and has three aspects:

- Renunciation arises from understanding suffering and its causes, and is the abandoning of desire and attachment.
- Renunciation, in turn, encourages goodwill toward others because we understand that they, too, live lives permeated by suffering and wish to find happiness.
- Goodwill inclines us toward harmlessness, and the wish that all beings be free from suffering.

We can train our mind by substituting Right Thought when negative thoughts arise.

**Right Speech** includes not lying, but instead cultivating truthfulness; not slandering others, but instead cultivating speech that promotes friendship and harmony; not shouting angry abuse, but instead cultivating courteous friendly speech; not gossiping or speaking mindlessly, but instead cultivating valuable important speech. Right Speech means we must be mindful whenever we speak and take care that what we say promotes happiness and avoids suffering.

**Right Action** is mindful behavior that does not harm others. The Buddhist precepts guide us toward Right Action. Not killing includes respecting the right of all beings to live their lives in search of happiness. We can refrain from mindlessly killing insects because all living beings have the potential to become enlightened. Not stealing includes cultivating honesty and respect for the possessions of others, and being satisfied with what we have. Not misusing the senses means not overindulging in sensual gratification, and appreciating the value of moderation. Not misusing intoxicants means either abstention or moderate use that does not lead to behavior that causes suffering.

**Right Livelihood** means making a living in an ethical way. Unfortunately, society encourages people to make a profit at the expense of ethics, so we need to choose our job carefully and not see money as the only criterion. Buddha taught that our money should be earned legally, nonviolently, harmlessly, and honestly. Useful jobs that help others, such as the caring professions, are ideal, but we can at least avoid working for companies that trade in arms, pollutants, and the suffering of humans or animals.

**Right Effort** is not about trying to make something particular happen. It is trying to be aware and mindful from moment to moment and to overcome laziness and negative behavior. Right Effort involves energy, which can be directed in positive ways such as generosity and compassion or in negative ways such as anger and desire. Our goal is to direct our energy toward wholesome states of mind. Buddha stressed the need for exertion and perseverance. He showed us the path to liberation but it is up to us to follow it.

**Right Mindfulness** is integral to meditation and facilitates the attainment of serenity and insight. The opposite of mindfulness is mindlessness—not thinking about the consequences of what we say or do, which can lead toward unnecessary suffering. Mindfulness trains us to be fully in the present and observe what arises without leaping to judgment and reaction. Living with our bare experience in the moment is Right Mindfulness, avoiding desire, idle dreams, and rigid thoughts.

**Right Concentration** develops a state of being calm and focused that prevents the mind from drifting into desire and aversion. Buddha taught that the ultimate purpose of right concentration is developing wisdom that will remedy ignorance, which is the basis for all suffering. Right Mindfulness and Right Concentration are both cultivated and developed in meditation. Right Concentration returns us to Right View at a higher level, because our fundamental misperception of how we exist obscures wisdom. In this way each point on the Noble Eightfold Path gradually purifies our mental obscurations and leads us toward enlightenment.

# buddhist meditation

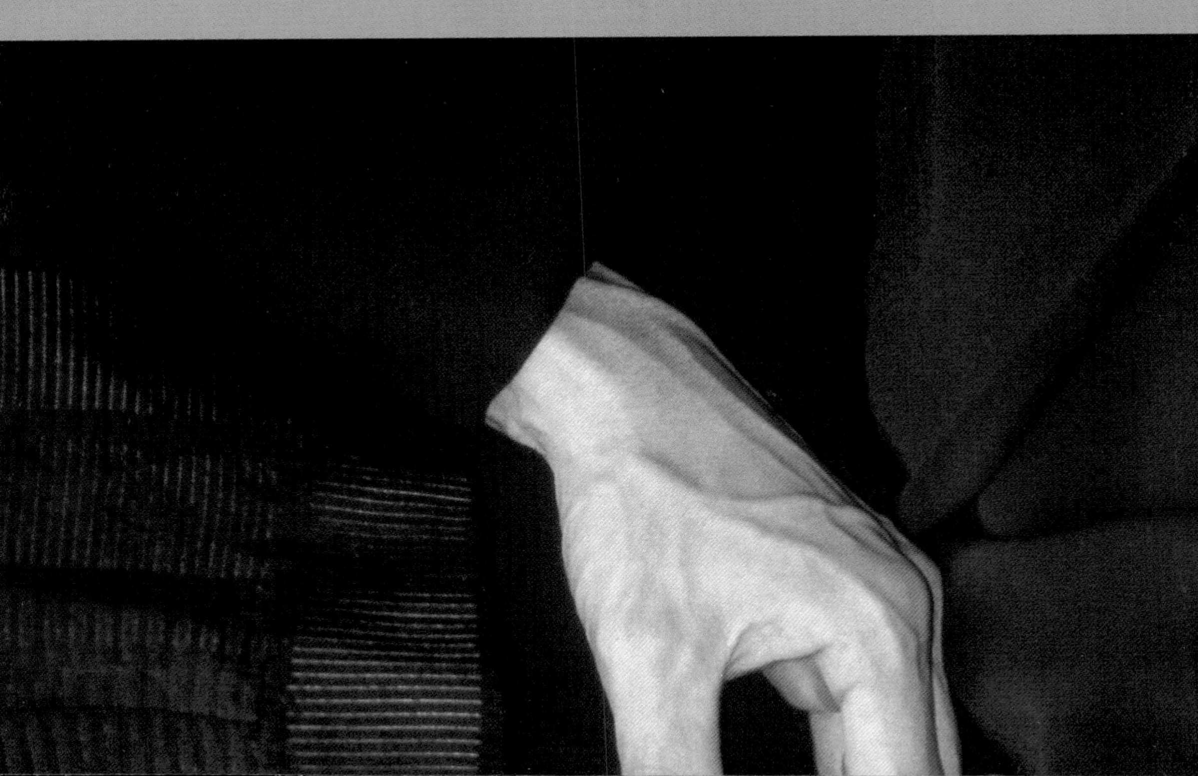

# what is meditation?

*The only requirement for meditation is the intention to be more awake, more aware, and to develop compassion and wisdom.*

MARTINE BATCHELOR

Meditation essentially involves withdrawing from the distractions of the external world to examine the inner world of the mind, bodily sensations, and feelings. The Tibetan word for meditation is *sgom*, which translates as "to become familiar with." This means that meditation requires continual, regular effort; the occasional sporadic attempt will not produce the desired result of calm awareness.

When we practice meditation we become familiar with the mind. This idea may seem strange because we use our minds all the time. However, we spend most of our time blindly following random thoughts, fantasies about the future, and nostalgic dreams of the past. These are simply the contents of the mind that we tend to follow without questioning the process. Meditation trains the mind to be aware of this process and to discover what lies beneath this apparently ceaseless mental chatter.

Meditation is not an attempt to suppress thoughts and feelings that naturally arise and pass. What we try to do is consciously observe this ongoing process. Through meditation we train the mind to maintain awareness of thoughts as they arise, recognize them as being transient and insubstantial, and decide not to follow them. Of course this is extremely difficult because our minds have wandered freely ever since we were conscious. But gradually, over time and with lots of practice, we begin to glimpse the nature of our mind that lies beneath our superficial thoughts.

We can perceive the mind as being like a deep ocean with hidden depths. Usually we are aware only of the waves on the top, which rise and break, like the thoughts that arise and pass on the surface of the mind. In the same way that waves are swallowed up into the vastness of the ocean, so thoughts are effortlessly absorbed back into our minds. When we meditate, we try to catch glimpses of the part of the mind that is like the ocean's hidden depths—what lies between the end of one thought and the beginning of another. This is the pure nature of the mind.

# benefits of meditation

*Peace of mind, mental tranquillity, may not necessarily be felt as a specific sensation, but can provoke a physical sensation of joy and happiness.*

H. H. THE DALAI LAMA

The ancient discipline of meditation has brought tranquillity, happiness, and wisdom to many persons from different cultures who have embarked on this inner voyage of discovery. Such wonderful benefits provide a good motivation to start meditating. The joy and happiness mentioned in the Dalai Lama's preceding statement cannot be found in material possessions. Buddhism teaches that all things are impermanent and subject to change, so there is no way any object, relationship, or life situation can provide lasting

satisfaction. Only within our own minds can we find the seeds for potential happiness, and meditation can bring these seeds to fruition.

Many people who live in the modern world suffer from high levels of stress. The pressures of finding and keeping a lucrative and satisfying job, together with the daily effort of commuting to and from work, take their toll. Relationships, or the lack of them, can cause emotional stress. Yet many of the leisure activities designed to ease the stress and tension of daily life are ineffective. They become other things to do, which can make stress increase instead of decrease. Meditation allows us to rest in simply being alive; there is nothing to do except be aware of thoughts, sensations, and feelings.

Yet meditation is not passive. On the contrary, the goal of meditation is to really be alive—to be present to each precious moment of life. Once the mental baggage of superficial thoughts has been cleared away, the mind is bright and vibrant—able to respond with clarity and creative imagination to whatever situation we encounter. Spaciousness of mind facilitates kindness and compassion both to others and to ourselves, and focused attention brings wisdom to deal with matters in a skillful way.

We can remind ourselves that the Buddha chose to sit in meditation—alone with his ongoing experience of life, from breath to breath—until he awakened. The ultimate purpose of meditation is to awaken to our own true nature, and this is the greatest benefit of all. We can all meditate in the attempt to awaken to our own true nature because meditation does not require special talent or great cleverness—simply an open mind and the willingness to keep practicing day after day.

# how to sit for meditation

*Sit straight and be straight in the practice.*

ZEN SAYING

The classic meditation posture involves sitting sit cross-legged on the floor on a meditation cushion, which is called a *zafu*. However, this is not always comfortable, and sitting on a firm chair with both feet on the floor provides a good alternative. When the body is relaxed but held upright, the body supports the mind and helps it to be clear and calm.

In terms of posture, the most important requirement is to keep a straight back. The body's natural energies circulate through the central nervous system in the spine. Maintaining a straight back allows these energies to flow freely, which facilitates a meditative state. The following instructions apply whether you are sitting on a meditation cushion or a chair:

- *Sit in a relaxed manner, not too stiff but not slumped over. Remember to keep your back straight.*

- *Incline your head slightly forward. Keeping your eyes half open, focused down at a gentle angle, helps prevent sleepiness. You should close your eyes, however, if keeping them open proves too distracting.*

- *Your head and face should be relaxed with your mouth gently closed and your tongue resting on the palate behind your upper teeth. This reduces the need to keep swallowing, which is a distraction.*

- *Keep your hands gently folded in your lap, palms facing upward with one hand on top of the other. Or rest one hand on each knee if you prefer.*

- *Try not to react immediately to discomfort, which will inevitably arise. If you observe the sensation without moving, sometimes the discomfort passes of its own accord. If discomfort changes to pain, adjust the body gently.*

Your meditation will benefit from assuming the correct posture at the beginning. It is difficult to rest in stillness because, although the body is motionless, the mind is as active as ever and thoughts continue to arise and pass. However, the body's stillness will eventually help the mind to become calm. This posture will feel more natural as it becomes more familiar, and you will begin to appreciate the advantage of sitting correctly.

# preparations for meditation

*Formal meditation means taking the time to meditate in silence.*

MARTINE BATCHELOR

There are two ways to prepare to meditate: inner motivation and resolve, and outer circumstances. Both are equally important. There is not much point in trying to meditate if you have not prepared yourself properly. It is a good idea to spend some time in ensuring that you are well prepared, not just rush into a meditation session and then discover something is not quite right.

Inner motivation is essential. You need to ask yourself, "Why am I going to meditate?" The immediate answer is to find some inner space, peace, and calm. These are tangible benefits that you will experience from meditation.

From the Buddhist perspective, it is necessary to have a deeper reason for meditating. This is based in the realization that although everyone wants to find happiness, it is dissatisfaction that is encountered most of the time. Meditating with the understanding that your own happiness is interrelated with that of others helps develop the motivation to wish sincerely that all beings find happiness.

When you start to meditate, you need to make the external surroundings as conducive as possible. Once you are more experienced you can meditate informally in any condition. But at the beginning and in formal meditation sessions you need to create a suitable environment.

• *A quiet room where you will not be disturbed for the duration of your meditation session is most important. Choose a location that is removed from other people, traffic, music, machinery, and so forth.*

• *Ideally the room will be light and airy. It is important to make sure the room is not so dark that you will fall asleep! A statue or painting of the Buddha near where you are sitting is a wonderful inspiration for your meditation.*

• *Remember to unplug or turn off your telephone.*

• *It is a good idea to set an alarm clock to alert you when your meditation session is finished. This will lessen the temptation to be constantly looking at the clock to see how much time has passed.*

# advice for beginners

*In the beginning it is best to meditate for short periods—ten to thirty minutes—and end your session while mind and body are still comfortable and fresh.*

KATHLEEN MCDONALD

It is easy to become discouraged after one or two sessions of meditation, because when you first begin to meditate your mind seems most resistant to doing what you want it to do. Instead of the peace and calm you hoped to experience, your mind seems more chaotic than ever. In fact what is in your mind is not much different than usual. What is happening is that you were previously unaware of the activity of the mind. Because it is easy to become disheartened, the following points will help you continue to meditate.

• *Make a commitment to yourself to meditate regularly for a month.*

• *The benefits of meditation will not be experienced fully if you meditate only occasionally, once a week or less.*

• *It is ideal to meditate every day, or at least five days a week. This schedule makes meditation an integral part of your life.*

*• Find a meditation teacher to help you, or even a friend who has some meditation experience. Although meditation is an internal process, the insights of an experienced teacher can be enormously helpful and keep you on the right track.*

*• Join a meditation group of like-minded people. These meditation friends can be supportive if you have problems with your meditation by offering constructive advice. Likewise, you will be able to help others as you become experienced.*

*• Try to find a time of day that allows you to meditate regularly and a space that is always available, rather than choosing different times of day and various places.*

*• The best times to meditate are early in the morning or before you go to sleep at night. In the morning the mind is clear and fresh from sleeping. In the evening the mind is tired and stressed, and meditation helps calm it before sleep.*

*• As the preceding quotation suggests, don't be too ambitious or have unrealistic expectations of achieving instant mental calm. If you start with shorter sessions of meditation you can gradually increase the time. This is better than overdoing it at the beginning, feeling discouraged, and giving up.*

# dealing with problems

*No matter how strong your resolve to be present and concentrated, it is difficult to keep the mind from wandering off into memories, plans or fantasies.*

STEPHEN BATCHELOR

The most common problem when you start to meditate is thinking you can't do it. The mind of a beginner is likely to wander off continually. When the bell rings at the end of your meditation, you realize with guilt that you have been thinking your thoughts nearly the whole time.

Gradually over time and with regular, frequent meditation sessions the mind calms down. Observing the rising of thoughts without slavishly following them becomes possible—some of the time at least. But the most important thing to remember is that meditation is the willingness to keep sitting down and trying to continue. It is not the fantasy of being able to control the mind when you first start. Other common problems are addressed below.

Sometimes you experience the opposite of having raging thoughts, and this dullness and lethargy can lead to dozing off. This is caused by the mind and body responding to another habitual pattern—when you become still and quiet, you are often preparing to sleep. Determine whether or not you have been meditating too long. If not, try reminding yourself of your motivation to meditate—the determination to awaken—and your resolve to remain alert.

If this doesn't help, practice walking meditation until the end of the session.

Physical discomfort can interrupt the meditation session. Beware of fidgeting, and focus your attention on the area of discomfort. Sometimes the feeling will then dissipate. If pain persists, carefully adjust your position and continue to sit still.

Meditation is powerful. You might notice unusual images arising in the mind, or your body may feel lighter or heavier than usual. These experiences are quite normal. Simply observe that such an experience has occurred and return your attention to the meditation.

Sometimes meditation brings up old painful memories and feelings that you had previously repressed. These can be powerful and disturbing. Try to observe them and let them go. If—as occasionally happens—you continue to feel disturbed, stop meditating. Talk to a meditation teacher or a friend with experience in meditation who can listen sympathetically and offer advice.

# mindfulness meditation

*Meditation works differently from conventional thinking—it conserves energy wasted in countless thoughts, stress, and resistance.*

CHRISTOPHER TITMUSS

Mindfulness meditation is known by various other names such as calm meditation, tranquil abiding, or awareness meditation. It is also called mindfulness of breathing because the object of attention is the breath. By focusing your attention on the breath, you become aware of the moment-to-moment process of breathing. You do not attempt to change the breathing in any way or judge it as shallow or deep. All you do is bring your attention to the process of breathing and keep it there.

When you become aware of your breathing, you feel in touch with your whole physical and mental continuum—all the little mental, physical, and emotional sensations that collectively create who you are. After some time, this awareness brings a deep feeling of peace and contentment, of resting in the wonder of being alive. You also gradually realize how precious and fragile this life force is, because if you stopped breathing for even a few minutes you would die.

We are not in charge of our breathing; our bodies breathe for us. This is one of the miracles of life: the body knows how to breathe without us being conscious of the process. Normally we take breathing for granted, but mindfulness of breathing meditation brings our attention right into the heart of being alive.

Once the mind has calmed down and found some peace through mindfully watching the breath come and go, you then turn your attention to the thoughts arising and passing in the mind. But how can something that sounds so simple be so difficult? You discover that you are not in control of your mind any more than you are in charge of your breathing.

You can gradually train your mind through meditation to gain some awareness of the mind's tendency to follow thoughts randomly. But trying to control the mind is doomed to failure because the mind is beyond any concept of control. Once you have meditated for a while, observing your thoughts arise and pass, your sense of self as a concrete entity dissolves. This is because you notice that your sense of self changes subtly from moment to moment. This is just a taste of the liberating freedom that meditation can bring.

# practice of mindfulness meditation

*Thoughts come and go; they are transient, momentary. Notice them and let them go, returning your attention again and again to the breath.*

KATHLEEN MCDONALD

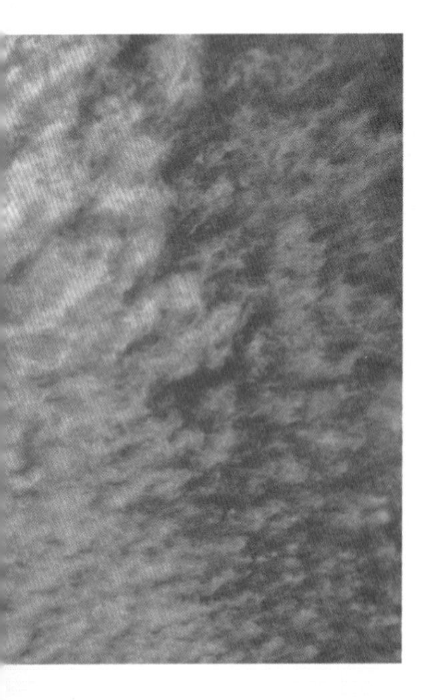

Try to practice meditation according to the following instructions as often as you can to derive the maximum benefit. Ideally, you could meditate once or even twice a day.

• *Sit on a chair or cushion in the meditation posture as described on page 46. It is a good idea to experiment with both positions to see which is more comfortable for you.*

• *Take a few moments to settle. Resolve to sit still for the entire meditation session.*

• *Make the commitment to meditate as well as you can, letting go of your thoughts, fantasies, and memories for the duration of the meditation.*

- *Set an alarm clock for ten minutes and then try to forget about the time. If this seems very short, try fifteen or twenty minutes next time. If it seems very long, persevere with ten-minute sessions.*

- *Bring your attention to your breathing by focusing either on the sensation of breath entering and leaving at the tip of your nostrils, or the sensation of the rising and falling of your abdomen. Try both, then stick with the method that suits you best.*

- *Be mindful that you are here now in the present moment and all you are doing is watching the breath.*

- *When a thought arises, be aware of it as just a thought. Let it go. You do not have to follow it, however attractive it might seem. You have made the decision to meditate for ten minutes and you can think all your thoughts afterward.*

- *Be aware that your mind will wander a lot when you begin meditating. Don't judge yourself harshly, but do keep on trying. Each time you notice you are following some thought or feeling, bring your attention gently back to the breath and try to keep it there.*

- *When the alarm sounds, slowly bring your attention to your surroundings. Do not rush off immediately. Instead, take some time to evaluate the experience. Resolve to meditate again soon and move thoughtfully into your daily life.*

# insight meditation

*You yourself must make the effort. Buddhas only point the way. Those who have entered the Path and who meditate will be freed from the fetters of illusion.*

THE DHAMMAPADA

The tranquillity you gain from mindfulness meditation is not sufficient in itself to lead you toward awakening. You also need the sharp incisiveness of inquiry, which is developed in insight meditation. Insight meditation is grounded in the calm, single-focused concentration you develop in mindfulness meditation, but it goes farther. Once you have gained some experience of mindfulness meditation, you can include periods of insight meditation to enhance your meditation practice.

The mind has an innate ability for perception and sustained analysis that you uncover after superficial mental chatter has stilled. Insight meditation involves looking deeply and inquiring into your thoughts and feelings as they arise. Instead of taking them for granted, you keep questioning and challenging your experience. Ultimately, insight meditation is more effective on the path to awakening because it uses your natural human intelligence and discriminating awareness to gain insight into your experience of being alive.

One of the main things we discover in insight meditation is how we are creatures of habit. We get stuck in habitual ways of responding and behaving,

which we continue to do mindlessly. When we examine these habitual behavioral patterns, we see that many of them are destructive or negative in some way. We end up doing something because we did it before, not because it is a thoughtful, appropriate response to the current situation. Insight into ourselves and our habitual behavior is liberating because it gives us the potential to change.

Insight meditation can also be used to analyze particular aspects of Buddhist philosophy, such as compassion. In this case you inquire into compassion, and bring to mind all the benefits of cultivating and practicing compassion. This logical reasoning helps deepen your understanding of why compassion is important. It also familiarizes the mind with the positive nature of compassion, which facilitates compassionate thoughts arising naturally.

Insight meditation brings self-knowledge, which we can use to help solve our problems by developing wisdom. When we keep inquiring into our experiences we start to see that everything we do and feel has a cause and also an effect. This helps us be less caught up in mindless behavior. We feel more spacious and able to choose how we react.

This journey of self-discovery is a radical confrontation with the contents of our mind, and is not always easy or pleasant. This is why we alternate our meditation method between mindfulness and insight; watching the breath is calming and inquiry heightens our experience. Together these meditations lessen stress, deepen concentration, and help you respond creatively and appropriately to your inner processes and the world around you.

# insight meditation practice

*We must train the mind to know the sense impressions and not get lost in them. To make it peaceful. Just this is the aim of all this difficult practice we put ourselves through.*

AJAHN CHAH

Whenever you practice insight meditation, it is helpful to calm the mind first with some time spent watching the breath come and go. Without the single-pointed concentration developed through mindfulness meditation, your insight meditation will not be so powerful or effective. Spend twenty minutes in your first session and increase the time gradually during subsequent meditation sessions until you can meditate without discomfort for fifty minutes.

• *Sit comfortably in the meditation posture (see page 46) and spend some time watching the breath.*

• *Gradually your mind will slow down and you can observe thoughts arising and passing. Start to inquire into your thoughts and feelings.*

• *Analyze what you are thinking and how you are feeling. Try to see where they come from, what is their cause, and what effect they might have.*

- *If your mind begins to wander and drift into fantasies, return to watching the breath. Once your concentration strengthens, return to inquiry and analysis.*

- *Try hard to penetrate a thought or feeling with your intellect and question what you habitually think you know about it. Allow your intuitive feelings to interact with your analysis; be creative, spacious, and open to new insights.*

- *You can think of insight meditation as an internal debate that questions all your assumptions and inquires into all possible interpretations and angles. You are not looking for definitive answers, so keep the questioning flexible and open.*

- *Insight meditation can be difficult, but don't worry. Doubts, questions, and old painful memories and feelings may arise. But stay with the process or, if you get distracted, return to watching the breath.*

- *When issues, difficult feelings, and doubts arise, look at them carefully and analyze them too. You can learn from anything and everything that arises during meditation.*

- *When the alarm sounds to alert you that your meditation has finished, spend a few minutes quietly watching the breath before you resume your daily activities.*

# walking meditation

*Walking meditation is an art! You are not going anywhere, you are walking just for the sake of walking.*

MARTINE BATCHELOR

Walking meditation is practiced slowly and contemplatively. The whole point is the bare experience of walking. The moving body is the focus of attention. Because you are walking so slowly, there is plenty of time to really feel the subtlety of each movement and to be completely present to the experience.

Walking meditation can be alternated with sitting meditation when you meditate for a long time, allowing the body to stretch and the mind to freshen. When you practice sitting meditation, you watch thoughts and feelings arise and pass. In walking meditation, lifting each foot and placing it down mindfully keeps you in touch with the flow of life. Try walking meditation for ten minutes and increase the time, if you like, in further sessions.

• *Walking meditation is done on a short path of 35–70 feet (10–20 meters). It can be done indoors or outside in nature, but be clear where the path starts and ends.*

*• Stand for a few minutes at the beginning of the walking path and watch the breath. Then start to walk slowly, being aware of picking up each foot and putting it down. Try to be aware of all the muscles and energies that are involved.*

*• You can coordinate each step with each breath if you like. This keeps the pace suitably slow.*

*• While you are walking, your arms should be folded over the abdomen or hanging loosely at your sides.*

*• Remember that you are not going anywhere; you are just walking.*

*• When you reach the end, stand for a few moments, turn around, pause, and be aware of standing. Then begin walking mindfully back along the path.*

*• If you become distracted, stand for a few moments and watch the breath until your mind calms and your concentration returns. Then slowly walk on.*

*• When you are ready to finish, continue until you reach one end of the walking path. Stand mindfully for a few moments. Then gently move into your daily life.*

# visualization meditation

*A mental image of the Buddha is recommended as the focus of attention in the development of single pointed concentration.*

KATHLEEN MCDONALD

There are several Buddhist meditations that involve visualization. As the preceding quotation indicates, you can use a visualized image of the Buddha to strengthen concentration. To do this, you interchange visualization of the Buddha with watching the breath. When the mind becomes dull, distracted, or excitable while watching the breath, switch to visualization. Alternating between these two methods is most effective. There is also a purification visualization in which you visualize your whole body as being made of light. This is effective for generating peace and harmony and for promoting deep relaxation.

There is a Tibetan Buddhist practice called *tantra* that uses extensive and detailed visualization. The main object visualized is a mandala; a sacred space or palace in which a Buddhist deity or Buddha resides. Various devotional practices of Buddhism also involve visualization, such as visualizing offerings of delightful objects to the Buddha. This is usually accompanied by reciting prayers and prostrating in front of an altar or image of the Buddha. A simple visualization meditation using the breath is described opposite.

- *Spend five minutes or so watching the breath in mindfulness meditation. Then decide to visualize the breath for the next three inhalations and exhalations before returning to simply watching the breath.*

- *As you breathe in, visualize the in breath as pure white light and say to yourself that you are breathing in and enjoying the love, wisdom, and compassion of the Buddha.*

- *As you breathe out, visualize the out breath as black smoke, and say to yourself you are breathing out and dispelling your anger, hatred, and self-cherishing or selfishness.*

- *Return to watching the breath for a few minutes; then repeat the three visualized in and out breaths.*

- *This easy practice is surprisingly powerful for developing positive qualities and letting go of negative ones. It also transforms the simple watching the breath mindfulness meditation into a purification meditation.*

- *This meditation is especially recommended if you feel angry, depressed, or otherwise emotionally unbalanced or disturbed.*

# informal meditation in daily life

*The practice of mindfulness . . . should be brought to bear on what is happening at any and every moment.*

JOHN SNELLING

Meditation is not an activity confined only to formal meditation sessions. We need to bring the quality of our meditation into our daily life to fully experience the benefits. In this way, mindfulness can help transform our lives. Instead of mindlessly reacting in habitual ways, like getting angry and frustrated in a traffic jam, we can remind ourselves that there is nothing inherently irritating about being stuck in traffic; it is only our reaction that causes the problem. Informal meditation helps us regard these situations as precious opportunities to be mindful and watch the breath.

Informal meditation is finding as much time as possible outside of our formal meditation sessions when we can remember to stay calm and mindful, watching the breath and not shouting angrily at someone because we are having a bad day. When we are angry our breathing becomes shallow and rapid, and we don't take enough oxygen into our bodies. This creates further physiological changes, such as increasing anxiety, and creates a vicious circle. Informal meditation is being mindful, catching yourself before you give in to expressing your negative feelings, taking deep breaths, and calming down.

The prime tool of meditation is our own mind, and as we are never apart from our minds we have plenty of opportunities for informal meditation. We can use informal meditation for pleasure, not just for calming anger and irritation. The experience of sitting beside a beautiful view and enjoying it is enhanced by watching the breath mindfully. This puts you in close touch with your bodily sensations and feelings so you are really present to the whole experience. This is a natural inclination for many people, but doing it consciously transforms the experience into something quite special and spiritual.

Walking in nature is another wonderful informal meditation. Instead of walking with your head down, lost in thought, try walking slowly, looking around at the trees and flowers, listening to all the little sounds of leaves crunching underfoot, birds singing, and so forth. Experience the smells of wet earth, sea air, or whatever arrives at your nostrils, and feel the warm breeze on your skin or the sudden chill of a gust of wind. Paying close attention to all your senses in this way calms the mind, deepens concentration, and uncovers underlying feelings and thoughts—just like the other meditations described. Informal meditation helps you live life fully in the here and now, appreciating every precious moment and not wasting life away in daydreams.

# buddhist traditions

# the spread of buddhism

*The essence of the Buddhist teachings does not change; wherever it goes, it is suitable.*

H. H. THE DALAI LAMA

The diversification into different schools of Buddhism resulted, in part, from the changes and developments that happened after the Buddha's *parinirvana*—his passing away from this world. A council of senior monks met shortly after the Buddha's death to decide what to do next. The Buddha had taught in the oral tradition common in India at that time. The monks carried this on, with recitation of the major teachings of the Buddha and the monastic code at regular intervals. It was not until around four hundred years after the Buddha's death that his teachings, called *suttas* or *sutras*, were actually written down.

After this time, Indian Buddhism went through many changes and interpretations, and eighteen major schools developed out of the Buddha's original teachings. Indian Buddhism was virtually wiped out in the thirteenth century by the invading Muslim conquerors. However, over the centuries, wandering Buddhist monks and teachers took Buddhist texts and philosophy to other countries. Whenever Buddhism traveled to a new land, it integrated with aspects of that country's indigenous religion. Buddhism today is the dominant established religion in several countries throughout Asia, with each country practicing its own culturally conditioned version.

Ceylon (modern-day Sri Lanka) was the first country to fully embrace Buddhism. Around 250 B.C.E. a Buddhist monk and nun visited Ceylon and were well received by the king, so Buddhism flourished. The Buddhism practiced in Sri Lanka is Theravada Buddhism, which is similar to the Indian Buddhism that was practiced during the Buddha's life. Theravada Buddhism also traveled to Thailand, probably in the third century, and is still practiced extensively there today. Burma (now called Myanmar) was influenced by both Theravada and Mahayana Buddhism in the fifth and sixth centuries, although Theravada prevailed. The current socialist Burmese government tolerates Buddhism, but the opposition leader Aung San Suu Kyi remains a devoted Buddhist. There were times when Buddhism also flourished in Laos, Indonesia, and Kampuchea (formerly Cambodia).

A new development in Indian Buddhism called Mahayana Buddhism occurred around the beginning of the Common Era. Mahayana Buddhism differs from Theravada Buddhism in that it replaces the spiritual ideal of personal liberation with the Bodhisattva ideal. The Bodhisattva, literally "enlightenment being," strives for liberation in order to help all other beings find liberation. This altruistic aspiration is called Bodhicitta, the mind of enlightenment, and reveals that Mahayana philosophy sees through the illusory boundary between self and others, regarding all beings as equal. Other theoretical differences exist, but both traditions share the essence of what the Buddha taught. In practice, all the Buddha's teachings can be summarized as not harming others, which is emphasized mainly in the Theravada tradition, and helping others, which is emphasized in Mahayana Buddhism.

In the first century B.C.E. Mahayana Buddhism traveled east from India along the Silk Road together with merchants trading in spices and silk. So China was exposed to Buddhism at this time, but it was not until 220 C.E. when the Han dynasty collapsed that Buddhism became popular. Buddhism flourished alongside Taoism and had a Golden Age between the sixth and ninth centuries. During this time various schools of Buddhism arose, notably Chan, or Chinese Zen. Buddhism then slowly declined, and was ravaged by the Communist and Cultural Revolutions of the twentieth century. Now, however, limited Buddhist practice is permitted.

Mahayana Buddhism spread to Afghanistan and Russia, but never became the prevailing religion. However, Chinese political dominance ensured that Mahayana Buddhism took root in Korea, where Zen then flourished. Vietnam was exposed to both Theravada and Mahayana Buddhism, and today Vietnamese Buddhism is predominantly Zen. Buddhism traveled from China into Japan in the sixth century. The practice of Buddhism was particularly prevalent in the tenth century when the two schools of Japanese Zen—Soto and Rinzai—arose. From the mid sixteenth century until Japan opened her doors to the world in 1868, Buddhism declined. Today both schools of Zen are practiced alongside Pure Land Buddhism and the lay-oriented Nichiren Soka Gakkai, both of which are discussed at the end of this chapter.

The great Indian Buddhists Shantarakshita and Padmasambhava took Buddhism to Tibet in the eighth century, although an earlier king had married two Buddhist wives. Buddhism was practiced alongside the indigenous Tibetan tradition of Bon, both traditions influencing each other. Buddhism was repressed in the ninth century, but in the eleventh century two more great Indian teachers—Atisha and Naropa—arrived. This heralded a Buddhist renaissance, despite Tibet falling under Mongol patronage. In the eighteenth century, China replaced the Mongol protectorate. This, however, remained a formality until the Chinese communist invasion in 1950, which violently destroyed much of Tibetan Buddhism. Currently Buddhism is permitted, but not encouraged, although Tibetan Buddhism flourishes in exile. Buddhism traveled to Mongolia, Sikkim, Ladakh, Bhutan, and Nepal. Although these countries adopted Buddhism, they did not make major innovations.

# theravada buddhism

*Theravada survives today as a living tradition in Sri Lanka, Burma, and Thailand, and it is from these countries that it has been transmitted to the West.*

JOHN SNELLING

Theravada Buddhism can trace its roots all the way back to the Sthaviravada school, one of the eighteen schools of Buddhism that developed in India after the Buddha's death. Theravada means "The way" or "Teachings of the Elders," and this tradition of Buddhism bears a close resemblance to the way the Buddha and his followers lived and practiced. The ancient language of Pali is still used by the Theravada Buddhists today to chant prayers, and Pali is the same language in which the collected teachings, or suttas, of the Buddha were first written down. These suttas are collectively called the Pali Canon, and are the main scriptures studied by the Theravada Buddhists.

In traditional Asian Theravada Buddhist countries such as Sri Lanka and Thailand, there is a clear demarcation between monastics and their lay supporters. There are many monasteries and thousands of monks, plus a smaller number of nuns. At first glance the monastic life appears rather austere, but in fact it provides a great freedom from material and family concerns. It also gives a sense of belonging to an ancient order of fellow Buddhists.

There are many monastic rules. Monastics are celibate and are not allowed to touch or handle money. They are also forbidden to store or cook food, so everything they eat must be given to them. Other than an optional light breakfast, monastics eat only one meal a day, which must be taken before noon. If a monk is traveling and does not find someone to give him food before noon, then he will not eat that day. A monk or nun is allowed very few possessions other than a spare robe, a needle and thread to mend robes and sandals, and an alms bowl.

The lay supporters provide administrative services. They also cook the daily meal, or they bring food in as a donation. Sponsoring a meal at the monastery earns the donor much spiritual merit. It is also a custom for the monks to go on alms rounds, so that the lay people can put food in the monks' begging bowls. In return for this material support, the monks provide spiritual and religious advice. They also conduct religious services as well as marriage, death, and birth ceremonies. In this way, there is a symbiotic and mutually supportive community in traditional Buddhist countries that serves everyone's material and religious needs.

Monastics tend to lean toward either scholarly or meditative pursuits. This is reflected in the two main structures of Theravada Buddhism. Large temples and monasteries, which are learned centers of study and debate, are usually found in towns and cities. Other monks devote themselves to intensive meditation in monasteries in remote natural settings, which are sometimes just a few huts in a forest clearing. However, both urban and rural monks share the same simple lifestyle of the traditional Buddhist monastic.

Theravada Buddhism has traveled to the West, but has been adapted somewhat to fit into a modern lifestyle and to accommodate the different needs of Westerners. There are a few traditional Theravada monasteries located in the Western world, including Amaravati in England and Abhayagiri in the United States. These Western Theravada Buddhist monasteries function in similar ways to their Asian counterparts. Many of the senior Western monks and nuns spent some years in monasteries in Thailand or Sri Lanka, which ensures that the traditions are kept purely. These monasteries offer Buddhist teachings, retreats, and spiritual advice for their lay supporters, which include Thai, Burmese, and Sri Lankan people living in the West.

However, the biggest Theravada Buddhist influence in the West is the prevalence of *vipassana* or "insight meditation." This meditation has proved popular and beneficial to a wide range of people, and there are many centers offering vipassana courses and retreats. This basic but profound meditation method is of great use to people living a hectic, stressful, modern lifestyle. Those who practice vipassana meditation typically keep a short daily practice and attend one retreat a year of ten days, or even a month. They might also visit a monastery on a major festival day. In this way, Theravada Buddhism as practiced in the West creates space for spiritual practice within the framework of daily life. Many people need to work to earn a living and have families and other commitments, yet still appreciate the benefits of regular meditation. Theravada Buddhism does make a distinction between pure spiritual and more secular activity. These are called, respectively, the Path of Liberation and the Path of Worldly Well-Being. In practice, these paths are not separate and reinforce each other. Yet this is a poignant reminder that the ultimate aim of Buddhist practice is liberation from the suffering nature of existence, and not just enabling Buddhist practitioners to live well in this world.

# meditation on lovingkindness

Metta *is a Pali word meaning "lovingkindness " or "friendship." It is part of the living tradition of Buddhist meditation practices that cultivates spaciousness of mind and openness of heart.*

SHARON SALZBERG

This is a popular meditation in the West. Sending out thoughts of lovingkindness toward the many suffering beings in the world is an active expression of compassion.

Sit comfortably in the meditation posture (see page 46). Spend a few minutes watching the breath. Bring to mind someone you love. Then, even as you let this person fade from consciousness, a warm, loving feeling will remain. In order to develop lovingkindness toward others, we need first to develop lovingkindness toward ourselves. Often we don't feel worthy, or we feel that we don't deserve to be happy. This meditation helps us accept ourselves as we are.

*• Silently repeat: "May I live safely and experience happiness, peace, and joy. May I have good health, and may my daily life flow easily without problems." You may vary these phrases to whatever is meaningful for you. What is important is to generate feelings of lovingkindness, not intellectual thoughts.*

*• After five to ten minutes, bring to mind someone who has helped you, such as a Buddhist teacher or friend. Repeat the phrases, substituting this person's name for your own. Generate deep feelings of lovingkindness toward this person.*

*• After another five to ten minutes, include a good friend in your thoughts and spend time generating feelings of lovingkindness toward this person. Then include a person for whom you have neutral feelings or indifference. This is a bit harder, so remind yourself that this person wants to find happiness and alleviate suffering, just like yourself.*

*• Finally include someone who has harmed you. This is hardest, so tell yourself that you don't have to like the person or condone their negative behavior. You can, however, develop lovingkindness toward them by not wishing them harm. Remind yourself that people who behave badly experience much suffering, so offering lovingkindness is a compassionate response to their behavior.*

*• End by including all beings everywhere, and dedicate any merit generated from this meditation to the happiness of all beings.*

# meditation on mindfulness of sensations

*Mindfulness . . . makes us accessible to depths of awareness and clear seeing into the way things are.*

CHRISTOPHER TITMUSS

The meditation practices of Theravada Buddhism emphasize awareness and mindfulness. These are based upon the teaching of the Buddha found in the *Satipatthana Sutta*, The Discourse on the Four Foundations of Mindfulness. The following meditation focuses on mindfulness of the body, and the arising and passing of sensations.

- *Sit comfortably in the meditation posture (see page 46). Observe the breath arising and passing, paying special attention to the sensations at the tip of your nostrils and the rising and falling of your abdomen. Practice like this for five or ten minutes, remembering to gently bring the attention back to the breath every time it wanders.*

- *Now begin the process of scanning your body and its sensations with mindfulness. Your mind is now more peaceful from watching the breath, but it is also important at this stage to keep your body as still as possible, sitting without fidgeting or moving.*

*• Start at the top of your head. Observe all the sensations without judging them. This develops choiceless awareness, which means that you don't become attached to pleasurable sensations, and you don't develop aversion to any pain, tension, or other unpleasant sensation.*

*• Move your attention slowly down to your neck, chest, shoulders, arms, and so on, until you have gone through every part of your body. Gradually you will become aware that all sensations are continually changing, but by not reacting to them, you can observe each sensation as it arises and passes. It is important not to react to the different sensations—merely observe them with an open, nonjudgmental mind.*

*• If your mind wanders, return your attention to the last part of your body in which you remember observing sensations. By not judging sensations, you gradually develop equanimity. It then becomes possible to watch discomfort arise and dissipate without reacting and changing position.*

*• Some sensations may be painful, while others may feel blissful. However, you can learn from this meditation that suffering comes from reaction to sensations, not from the sensations themselves.*

*• Conclude the meditation with mindfulness of breathing for a few minutes.*

# zen buddhism

*When at last in a single flash you attain full realization,*
*you will only be realizing the buddha-nature*
*that has been with you all the time.*

HUANG-PO

This quote from the sixth-century Chinese Zen master poetically sums up the Zen Buddhist path. The whole purpose of practicing Zen is to see directly into, or awaken to, your own self nature. All other activities and endeavors are regarded as a waste of time. The essence of Zen is complete simplicity and directness. This stark approach encourages awakening in the moment, in the here and now. This is different from some of the other Buddhist traditions that encourage the gradual development of enlightenment by earning spiritual merit and practicing meditation for many years.

The Zen tradition emphasizes intensive meditation rather than study or ritual, though Buddhist principles inform and guide the practice. Zen is known for the bizarre behavior of Zen masters, strange and cryptic sayings called *koans*, and idiosyncratic stories. Such attributes can appear distinctly non-Buddhist at times—for example, a Zen master shouting at or striking one of his disciples. There is even a Zen story in which a disciple chops off his arm in order to impress his master. However, these actions are designed to startle us out of our usual thought patterns and behavior. They are actually skillful actions arising from the master's compassion to help his disciples wake up.

An amusing contemporary encounter between a renowned Zen master and an equally renowned Tibetan master illustrates the sudden and direct confrontational style of Zen. The two masters were to meet for the first time and their Western disciples eagerly anticipated the wonderful Buddhist debate that would ensue. However, when the Zen master entered the room of the Tibetan master he dispensed with any greeting. Snatching up an orange from a fruit bowl on the table, he thrust it under the Tibetan master's nose and demanded, "What is this?"—a well-known Zen koan. The rather startled Tibetan master turned to his main disciple and replied: "What's the matter? Hasn't he ever seen an orange before?" Should you ever encounter a Zen master, it is as well to be prepared for the unexpected.

As you saw with Theravada Buddhism, the monastic lifestyle prevails in traditional Asian Buddhist countries where Zen is practiced. Zen monasteries were often situated in remote mountainous places where there was little to disturb the intensive meditation and being close to nature. A few of these places still exist in China and Japan, but these days most Zen monasteries are more accessible and their occupants have regular interaction with lay devotees. In Korean Zen monasteries, intensive three-month meditation retreats are followed by three months of working in the fields; the essence of Zen is still simplicity.

Zen Buddhism developed when the sixth-century Indian monk Bodhidharma traveled to China and challenged the rather overly scholastic

Buddhism he encountered there. Bodhidharma regarded Zen as nothing more than "A direct pointing to the human heart and the realization of Buddhahood." Chan—Chinese Zen—eventually declined in China, but it went to Japan and flourished. Two main schools of Japanese Zen, adapted from the original Chan, still survive.

Dogen founded Soto Zen, which emphasizes intensive sitting meditation called *shikantaza*. Meditators traditionally sit facing the wall and are encouraged to think of themselves as Buddhas when they meditate, not just potential Buddhas. Rinzai was founded by Eisai and also practices sitting meditation. The major practice, however, is koan meditation in which meditators continuously ask themselves a question. There are no real answers to koans; the questioning is designed to bypass conceptual thought and, by breaking this habitual way of thinking, to awaken.

Westerners have been attracted by the direct simplicity of Zen and there are numerous Zen centers in many Western countries. Some are small and in out-of-the-way places, sometimes just a room where the group meets to meditate. Others are large residential Zen retreat or training centers like Throssel Hole in England, or Rochester Zen Center in the United States. Many centers have an integrated approach, combining elements of both Soto and Rinzai Zen.

Zen students living in a Zen center will rise early. Periods of meditation are typically interspersed with work periods throughout the day. More intensive meditation is practiced in regular retreats, called *sesshin*, and there are interviews with the master. During these interviews, called *dokusan*, the master will ask questions to determine how far the student has progressed, and may suggest working with another koan or intensifying the sitting meditation.

Zen practitioners try to cultivate the traditional Zen Three Attitudes of Great Faith, Great Courage, and Great Questioning. Great Faith means developing real belief and trust in our own Buddha Nature, believing that this does not exist anywhere outside of ourselves. Great Courage refers to the strength and staying power required to keep on the Zen path, which can be extremely challenging. Great Questioning is also known as Great Doubt, and refers to the inspiration to keep on sitting and questioning, not being satisfied with anything less than awakening.

# koan meditation

*Zen questioning uses koans . . . as a starting point for meditative inquiry.*

MARTINE BATCHELOR

Koan meditation combines concentration with inquiry. The koan is the essence of the meditation, bringing you back time and again to the present moment. In that instant you develop awareness of everything as you ask the question sincerely. The following koan meditation can help you uncover your own buddha nature.

• *Sit comfortably in the meditation posture (see page 46) and watch the breath for five minutes to calm the mind.*

• *Remind yourself that you are trying to awaken to your true nature using the method of repeatedly asking a question that resonates through the core of your being.*

• *One of the most popular koans is "What is this?" Start to ask the question silently in your mind. You can coordinate asking the question with your breathing, which gives an organic rhythm to your inquiry, by asking "What is this?" with every inhalation.*

*• Remember that you are not trying to answer the question; there is no conceptual answer. The whole point of the meditation lies in the questioning.*

*• Reflect that though you could ask "Who is this?" you stay with "What is this?" because you are trying to shake off your usual self identity, to discover who you are beneath your habitual ideas.*

*• Try not to speculate intellectually; stay with the question and keep repeating it silently with every breath.*

*• Be aware that irritation might arise—"I don't care what this is!"—but keep asking the question and the irritation will pass.*

*• If a sense of the mystery of life arises, rest in this until the mind wanders. Then return to the koan, but be careful not to get lost in thoughts and fantasies.*

*• In this moment, here and now, there is only one thing that exists: the question: "What is this?"*

*• Remember that you are not trying to make conventional sense of the koan. Watch what arises in your mind, however bizarre those thoughts might be. But let them go; they are not the point of the meditation.*

*• Finish the meditation with a few minutes of watching the breath. However, keep the question with you as you go about your daily life.*

洞山和尚、因僧問、如何是佛。山云、麻三斤。

# zazen meditation

*In Zazen neither intention, analysis, specific effort, nor imagination take place. It's enough just to be without hypocrisy, dogmatism, arrogance—embracing all opposites.*

TAISEN DESHIMARU

Zazen dispels the duality of practice and realization with the idea that when you sit you are already a Buddha. This paradoxical concept is typical of Zen, and how it breaks down the illusions that prevent us from awakening. It is said that many people burst out laughing at the moment of awakening. This is because enlightenment is already present, staring us in the face—we just don't realize it.

• *Sit mindfully in the meditation posture (see page 46) and watch the breath for five minutes to calm the mind. You might like to sit facing the wall, as this is traditional in Soto Zen meditation, but sit in your usual place if you prefer.*

• *Zazen is awareness practice, so simply become aware of your thoughts and how these arise and pass.*

• *Cultivate awareness of your body and what it is feeling, but do not become distracted by pain or pleasant sensations.*

*Try allowing all bodily sensations just to be; remember that you don't have to react to them. In this way pain may dissipate of its own accord.*

- *Do not try to control or suppress thoughts, but be mindful not to get caught up in them. If you become distracted, simply return to being aware.*

- *Do not judge your thoughts and feelings as good, bad, or neutral. Just be aware of everything as it arises and passes.*

- *You might experience momentary gaps between thoughts, which is pure awareness. But the minute you think this, you lose it. Try to be aware without thinking; this is how pure awareness is traditionally described.*

- *Being fully present in the moment is true awareness. True awareness is not letting the mind rest anywhere, as the moment the mind rests thoughts arise.*

- *Reflect that the mind is like a mirror. It reflects thoughts with clarity, but the mind is not the thoughts themselves.*

- *Finish the meditation by watching the breath, and try to maintain awareness as you move into other activities.*

# tibetan buddhism

*Tibetan Buddhism uses many different meditation methods, such as systematic reflection on death, visualization of mandalas, recitation of mantras, and* Dzogchen *(great completion).*

MARTINE BATCHELOR

Tibetan Buddhism, like everything in Tibet, was almost entirely hidden from the rest of the world until the last century. This enabled the Tibetans to create a wonderful, spiritually rich Buddhist culture that remained largely unchanged for many years. Tibet, perhaps more than any other Buddhist country, embraced Buddhism to such an extent that there was little in the way of life that was not colored by Buddhist beliefs. Their self-imposed isolation from the rest of the world created the ideal context in which Buddhism could evolve uninterrupted by outside influences.

After the establishment of Buddhism in the eighth century, huge monasteries developed that eventually housed one quarter of the male population. Nunneries existed, but to a lesser extent. Nuns and nunneries were not held in such high esteem, although almost every family contributed a child to the monastic system.

Not all the monks and nuns were brilliant students of Buddhism. But there were valuable roles for everyone because there were many everyday, domestic tasks that also needed to be fulfilled for the monastery to flourish. The monasteries were centers of learning and culture as well as of religious study and practice. Tibetan monks often studied medicine and astrology, art and sculpture, literature and poetry alongside Buddhist philosophy, although all these subjects were informed by Buddhist beliefs. Elaborate rituals and ceremonies were undertaken regularly, often taking many weeks to prepare. The lay people were mostly deeply religious, reciting mantras and religious texts as they went about their daily lives.

All this ended with the Chinese invasion of Tibet in 1950 and the systematic repression and destruction of the Buddhist way of life. This was exacerbated by the excessive brutality of the Cultural Revolution from 1966 to 1976, and the virtual eradication of centuries of Buddhist culture. Many Tibetans fled into exile to India, especially after the Dalai Lama's flight in March 1959. The Tibetans have gradually rebuilt some of their great monasteries in exile in India and continue to study and practice Buddhism as a way of life.

Tibet's tragedy allowed other cultures to have access to Tibetan Buddhism, and these days there are Tibetan Buddhist centers and monasteries throughout the Western world. Some Westerners have been ordained as monks

and nuns, and undertake serious study and lengthy meditation retreats in Western or Indian monasteries. The majority, however, remain lay students. Many maintain a daily meditation practice and attend a Buddhist center regularly for teachings from a Tibetan master, who is called a *lama*. There are four main schools of Tibetan Buddhism: Nyingma, Kagyu, Sakya, and Gelugpa. All share a basic theology based on Mahayana Buddhism. Nyingma lamas are often married and there is less emphasis on monasticism. The Nyingma school is the oldest, and influenced by the indigenous Bon tradition of Tibet. A particular teaching of the Nyingmas is Dzogchen, meaning Great Perfection or Completion, which has become popular among Westerners. Dzogchen has a directness similar to Zen, and is concerned with recognizing the primordial buddha nature within each individual's own intrinsic nature.

The Sakya tradition is least well known today, although the head of the

Sakyas, the forty-first Sakya Trizin, is a well known and highly regarded teacher. The Kagyus are also influenced by Bon, and the famous Tibetan saint Milarepa was a Kagyu practitioner. The Gelugpa was the last school to emerge. The great fourteenth-century monk Je Tsongkhapa started a reform movement that aimed at synthesizing the major teachings of the other schools. It emphasizes purity, monasticism, and study rather than the magical and ritual approach of the other schools.

The role of the lama in Tibetan Buddhism is fundamental, and guru devotion is the formal expression of the students' commitment to their teacher. This is based on recognizing buddha nature in all the lama's behavior, which is an inspiration to cultivate buddha nature themselves. There are two main levels in Tibetan Buddhism: Sutra and Tantra. Students start with the Sutra path, which includes simple calming of the mind and insight meditations, together with study of the Buddhist sutras, or scriptures. They also attend Buddhist ceremonies, called *pujas*, and are encouraged to listen to the lama's teachings as much as possible.

Once students have spent some years practicing the Sutra Path, they can move onto the mystical, ritualistic aspect of Tibetan Buddhism, called Tantra. In Tantra, the student visualizes a deity, such as Avalokiteshvara, the Buddha of Compassion, within the sacred palace the deity resides, called a mandala. Ritual implements such as bells and drums are held and rung at specific points in the rituals. Tantra is known as the quick path to enlightenment, but it takes many years before a student is ready to embark on the Tantric Buddhist path.

# meditation on our precious human rebirth

*Human existence is very precious,*
*but normally we fail to appreciate it.*

KATHLEEN MCDONALD

This is an excellent meditation if you are feeling depressed, inadequate, or hopeless. It helps you appreciate your good fortune in being alive, and in having the opportunity to realize your spiritual potential. By following the Buddhist path you can eventually awaken and discover true happiness.

- *Relax into the meditation posture (see page 46), and begin with watching the breath until your mind is calm.*

- *Bring your attention to how you feel about yourself. Check out your feelings honestly about your life and lifestyle, personality and behavior, and accomplishments and skills.*

- *Reflect that although you may feel content and happy at the moment, you can recall times when you were depressed; or that if you feel negative now, you can recall times of happiness. Be aware that moods change, so your moods are not the essence of who you are.*

- *Analyze your feelings about yourself. Do you feel areas of inadequacy, depression, or hopelessness? Are you satisfied with how you are, or do you feel worthless in some way?*

- *Make the resolve to seek happiness actively by relinquishing negative feelings of hopelessness, inadequacy, etc.*

- *To help you appreciate how fortunate you are, make some comparisons with others. Imagine being an animal with little control over life, driven only by desires to eat and procreate and having no opportunity for spiritual growth.*

- *Look at the life of a street beggar who has nothing to eat but has to beg all day and is scorned by others. The beggar has no time for anything other than the desperate attempt to survive.*

- *When you compare your problems with the misfortunes of others, you realize how fortunate you really are. You even take something like having eyesight for granted, but imagine how precious this would be to someone who is blind.*

- *Rejoice in your good fortune. Determine to make the most of life's opportunities, and have compassion for those less fortunate. Reflect that the opportunity to practice a spiritual path is ultimately more rewarding than material gratification.*

- *Finish with mindfulness of breathing, and rejoice in each breath.*

# meditation on the nature of mind

*Imagine that your mind is like a calm, clear lake, or a vast, empty sky; ripples appear on the surface of the lake and clouds pass across the sky, but they soon disappear without altering the natural stillness.*

KATHLEEN MCDONALD

When we meditate on the pure, clear nature of mind we can see directly into the transient nature of all our thoughts, feelings, and perceptions. This weakens our tendency to identify with our thoughts. Being less caught up in our thoughts leads to a softer, more spacious sense of being.

- *Sit and watch the breath for five minutes to calm the mind. Make sure you are breathing without thinking about breathing.*

- *Bring your attention to your consciousness or mind, and focus on the essential clarity of your consciousness.*

- *Imagine that you are lying on top of a hill looking up into the vast, clear blue sky above. This is like the nature of mind—spacious and clear. Clouds drift across the sky like thoughts drift across the mind. They are temporary and, if you focus on the clear space of mind, you can watch the thoughts drift away.*

*• Be aware that your consciousness is whatever is going on in your experience at this moment—all the thoughts, feelings, sensations, and sounds. Remind yourself that the essence of all these is pure, formless clarity. It is your reactions and judgments that obscure and color the bare awareness of these phenomena.*

*• Watch as your thoughts arise effortlessly. You do not have to reject or repress them, nor do you have to follow them. Your thoughts have no real meaning. They are insubstantial and have no power to obscure the clear nature of mind—unless you get caught up in following them or reacting to them.*

*• Simply observe the infinite, empty spaciousness of consciousness, and remember not to speculate about it. The purpose of the meditation is simply to experience the nature of mind.*

*• Finish by watching the breath. Try to keep the spacious quality of mind with you as you go about your daily life.*

# other buddhist traditions

*The devotional cults in particular brought Buddhism within reach of the ordinary man and woman.*

JOHN SNELLING

The three traditions of Buddhism looked at earlier in this chapter are the main schools of Buddhism today. However, throughout the history of Buddhism other schools developed, had moments of popularity, and then faded away or were absorbed into one of the other Buddhist schools. There are, however, two devotional schools of Buddhism that still attract devotees today. As the quotation suggests, they have always been popular with ordinary—usually poor—people.

Pure Land Buddhism is derived from the cult of Amitabha Buddha in China and Japan during the thirteenth century. The central tenet of Pure

Land is that because we live in a degenerate age it is futile and arrogant to assume that we can attain liberation through our own efforts. It matters not how much we strive in the study of Buddhist texts, nor how long we sit in meditation, in the quest to awaken from the Pure Land perspective.

Primarily a devotional practice, Pure Land teaches that we can attain liberation only by letting go of our personal spiritual ambitions and surrendering to the infinite mercy and grace of Amitabha, the Buddha of Infinite Light. The practice is based on reciting the name of Amitabha, or chanting his mantra. This is called the Nembutsu and is as follows: Namu-Amida-butsu. Pure Land practitioners recite this under their breath informally all day long, and may also chant formally in front of a statue of Amitabha once or twice a day.

Nichiren Shoshu is very popular in the West, with famous adherents such as Tina Turner giving the school a high profile. Nichiren was founded in thirteenth-century Japan by a fisherman called Nichiren Daishonin. He believed the Lotus Sutra, alone of the Buddhist texts, held the key to salvation. He did not particularly encourage study of the Lotus Sutra, instead believing that the essence was encapsulated in the title.

Practitioners chant Namu-myoho-renge-kyo, which means Homage to the Lotus Sutra. This is done twice a day in front of a copy of the Dai Gohonzon, the original mantra written down by Nichiren. In the beginning, practitioners are encouraged to chant for material objects. When they succeed, they develop faith in the spiritual power of the mantra. Then they are encouraged to chant for spiritual fulfillment and eventual awakening.

# towards a western buddhism

*Gradually in time there may be a Buddhism combined with Western Culture.*

H. H. THE DALAI LAMA

Buddhism flourishes in the West with many centers and monasteries of all the main Buddhist traditions established throughout the Western world. The label of "the fastest growing religion in the West" has also been applied to Buddhism. There is even an international Buddhist group founded by Sangharaksita in the 1960s called the Friends of the Western Buddhist Order (FWBO). The FWBO have developed an organization and teaching program based on Buddhist principles and meditation that also draws on Western literature and art. But there is nothing tangible that you can point a finger at and say definitively, "This is Western Buddhism."

As we have seen through the brief history of the major Buddhist traditions, it takes many hundreds of years for Buddhism to really establish itself in a meaningful way in a particular country. Buddhism may be the fastest growing religion in the West, but it remains at this stage peripheral to mainstream Western culture, and it is likely to remain there for the foreseeable future. Western society generally remains more interested in material consumption and gratification than in spiritual pursuits, especially an Eastern religion. Yet this is an exciting time for Western Buddhists as we try to create meaningful engagement between Buddhist beliefs and principles and Western society and culture.

In addition to Buddhist centers and monasteries that are dedicated to offering Buddhist teachings, meditation classes, and meditation retreats, Buddhist practice also influences how people live. Buddhists often try to find ways of using Buddhist ideals in practical ways to be of benefit to others, animals, and the environment. This is reflected in the adoption of an ecological, ethical lifestyle. Some Western Buddhists also incorporate Buddhism into their professional or charitable work, and Buddhism contributes to interfaith dialogue to create a greater understanding between the world's religions.

One area that has attracted much interest is the ongoing dialogue between Buddhism and psychotherapy. Western psychotherapy works with an individual's deepest feelings, fears, and hopes. This is essentially a spiritual path—though in the most general, non-denominational way that is unique to each person. Yet there are patterns of behavior that we all share, and Buddhist psychotherapy has a great deal to offer in helping people transform their problems and themselves, as well as finding meaning in their lives. There may not yet be a Western Buddhism, but there is certainly Buddhism in the West.

# devotional buddhism

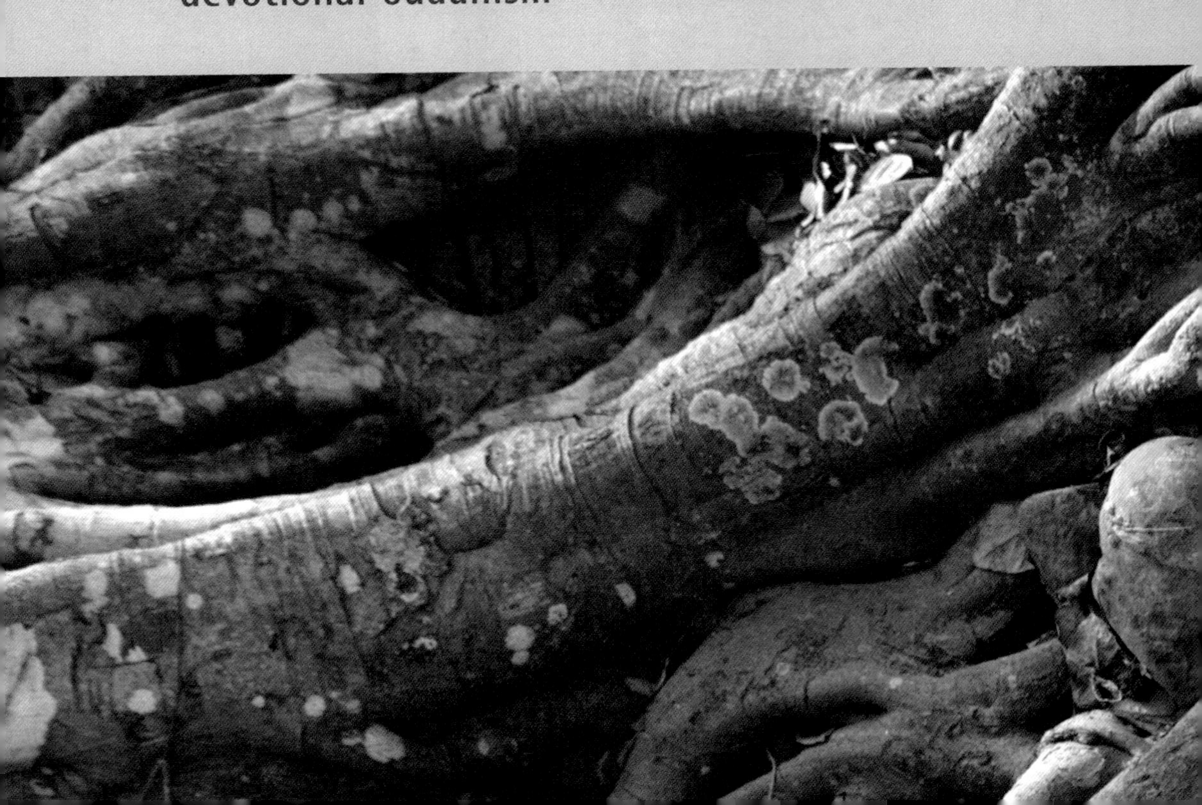

# developing faith in buddhism

*Faith is not equivalent to mere belief. Faith is the condition of ultimate confidence that we have the capacity to follow the path . . .*

STEPHEN BATCHELOR

When people first start to practice Buddhism, it is because they have faith that what the Buddha taught is effective and will help them to eventually awaken. In this way, faith is what leads them to start practicing Buddhism and meditating. This level of faith is primarily intellectual, based on a set of beliefs. You believe Buddhist meditation and philosophy will be beneficial because you have listened to Buddhist teachings, or read books, or heard other people say that meditation is beneficial. Once you feel convinced that it is a good thing to do, you try it. This is the beginning of faith.

When you start to actually meditate, your faith goes beyond the intellectual into the experiential. Every time you meditate, listen to Buddhist teachings, or attend a Buddhist ceremony, these become acts of faith. This means having confidence in your buddha nature and trusting your own potential to awaken. Your faith has been transformed from being outside of yourself to being inside yourself. Your faith is no longer simply in words, in your intellectual understanding, or in your idea of Buddha as some historical or metaphysical figure. Your faith is the willingness to sit and meditate, to inquire into the mystery of life that has brought you here at this time. Your meditation is an act of faith that you trust will one day help you awaken.

Faith is the foundation of Buddhist practice and meditation. Faith helps you keep going when you suffer setbacks, feel depressed, or fear that your meditation isn't getting you anywhere. Faith gives you the strength to move beyond difficulties. You continue to practice because each new circumstance you encounter and each new moment in meditation contains the potential for radical transformation. The next moment could be the moment of awakening.

Faith is inspirational. When we see someone with great faith bow down to a statue of Buddha or light incense and offer it on an altar, we know that this is not a mechanical ritual but a deeply devotional act of worship. This inspires our own faith.

# devotion to the buddhist teacher

*To meet a perfect teacher is more valuable than gaining a kingdom. Look at how those with no devotion treat the teacher as their equal!*

PATRUL RINPOCHE

The Buddhist teachings encourage you to find a teacher who can help you follow the Buddhist path and avoid mistakes, as well as guide you toward an in-depth understanding of Buddhist philosophy. The ultimate teacher is your own buddha nature, but you need an outer Buddhist teacher to help you discover the inner teacher. It is therefore important to cultivate devotion toward your teacher, and it is equally important to understand what devotion really is.

Some Western Buddhist students are uneasy with devotion and may have an inappropriate relationship with their Buddhist teacher. They may have a disrespectful attitude and lack trust in the teacher's words and actions. Or they may go to the other extreme and be mindlessly devoted to the teacher, abdicating all personal responsibility and relying on the teacher to make every little decision in life. The Buddha's middle way approach is best. This involves acting with great respect and devotion toward Buddhist teachers, but not relinquishing common sense. It is important to remember that your own buddha nature is the ultimate teacher.

A good Buddhist teacher is someone with integrity who can help show you the way through his or her teachings, attitude, and behavior. Traditionally in Buddhism a student finds one special teacher with whom they spend many years studying and practicing. This system doesn't always work in the modern world. Unless you become a serious Buddhist practitioner and find a teacher who is willing to take you on as a student in this manner, it is a good idea to listen to several Buddhist teachers from within the different traditions. This can also help you decide which tradition best suits your disposition.

Teachers who are monastics are traditionally accorded formal devotional respect. Should you have the opportunity to meet such a teacher you should ask someone to show you the correct greeting, which is usually a bow from the waist with hands folded at the heart. You should be mindful at all times to behave respectfully toward Buddhist monastics. This is because monks and nuns have dedicated their entire lives to practicing Buddhism. Although you are respectful to the teacher's person, you are ultimately honoring their great learning and understanding that is the manifestation of Buddha's teaching.

# auspicious days and buddhist celebrations

*Temple festivals, like the Lantern Festival, the Festival of the Buddha's Birthday, and All Soul's Festival, were great occasions for collective celebrations in which all strata of society took part.*

JOHN SNELLING

Throughout the calendar year there are various dates that are considered particularly auspicious for Buddhist practice or for holding specific ceremonies and festivals. Some of these are associated with a particular Buddhist tradition, while others are important days in the overall Buddhist calendar that commemorate such important events as Buddha's enlightenment. As the preceding quotation indicates, these are occasions for everyone in the Buddhist community to come together and participate in the religious ceremonies and general festivities. Buddhist teachings are also given to the large gathering by one of the leading Buddhist teachers.

In traditional Buddhist countries and in traditional monasteries in the West, these occasions are opportunities for lay people to make offerings to the monks and nuns. In the Theravada tradition, for example, the annual Kathina Festival heralds the end of the three month Rains Retreat. During Kathina the laity traditionally offer cloth for the monastics' robes. General

support and supplies for the monastery, such as food or money, is also offered on festival days.

Tibetan Buddhism has many auspicious days for different Buddhist practices throughout the year, and also has some major festivals. The Great Prayer Festival, or Monlam Chenmo, used to be held in Lhasa just after the Tibetan New Year, or Losar, with celebrations lasting a full three weeks. This is celebrated in lesser style by Tibetans in exile, but was prohibited in Tibet by the Chinese. Zen ceremonies include Bodhidharma Day which honors Bodhidharma, the First Zen Patriarch and founder of the Zen tradition. There is also the Jukai ceremony, which is for taking the Buddhist precepts for refraining from killing, stealing, and so forth.

Auspicious dates are also a good opportunity for personal practice. A Buddhist practitioner may spend the whole day meditating or may take certain Buddhist vows or precepts for the day, or even for a week or a month. Devotional practices such as prostrations in front of an image of the Buddha are also often performed, as well as making elaborate offerings to the Buddha in a temple or on a personal altar. In this way Buddhist festivals and auspicious days create a special time for practice and reflection.

# wesak the major annual buddhist festival

*The fifteenth of the month (Saga Dawa) when the moon is in the constellation of Saga [Taurus] commemorates the Enlightenment of the Lord Buddha and also his death and attainment of nirvana. It is perhaps the holiest day in the Buddhist calendar . . .*

HUGH RICHARDSON

Wesak—also known as Vesak in Sri Lankan, Saga Dawa or Sakadawa in Tibetan, Vaisakha Puja in Thai, or even just Buddha Day—is the most important festival in Buddhism, venerated equally by all the Buddhist traditions. This means that Buddhists from the different traditions often get together to celebrate Wesak under the auspices of an umbrella organization, such as the local Buddhist Society, in addition to holding their own tradition-based ceremonies.

Wesak is the celebration of Buddha's Birth, Enlightenment, and Parinirvana (his passing away), and is held on the full moon in May of every year.

Buddhists often devote themselves entirely to religious practices for the whole day, including meditation, saying prayers, reciting mantras or chanting from the Buddhist texts, prostrations, making offerings, and circumambulation of sacred sites and temples. It is reputed that the spiritual merit from whichever of these various spiritual practices is performed on this day is greatly multiplied. This means that the time remaining on the path to awakening is reduced for the Buddhist practitioner who undertakes intensive Buddhist practice on Wesak.

The Buddhist monasteries and temples perform special ceremonies. Some, such as those in the Tibetan tradition, can be extremely elaborate, while Zen and Theravada ceremonies tend to be simpler. It is traditional during Wesak for the laity to make offerings to the monks and nuns. Participation in Wesak festivities involves religious ceremony, but it is also a joyous, festive occasion. A special meal may be prepared at the monastery, or people may picnic in the temple grounds or in parks nearby. The Wesak Festival is for everyone in the Buddhist community, and whole families often spend the day at their local monastery or temple.

Wesak is celebrated in Western Buddhist monasteries and centers, often as a major event hosted by the Buddhist Society of individual Western countries. As well as celebrating Wesak, these are joyous occasions when all Buddhists—Westerners as well as immigrant Thai, Sri Lankan, Burmese, and Tibetans—can meet in the spirit of festivity and a shared spiritual path. This opportunity is particularly important in Western countries where Buddhists remain a minority.

# theravada refuge prayer

*Going for Refuge gives a continual perspective on life by referring one's conduct and understanding to the qualities of* Buddha *(wisdom),* Dhamma *(truth), and* Sangha *(virtue).*

AJAHN SUMEDHO

Taking refuge with a Buddhist teacher means formalizing your commitment to the Buddhist path. Most Buddhist teachers suggest you spend time listening to Buddhist teachings, meditating, and talking to other Buddhists before requesting the Three Refuges. This is to ensure that you have thoroughly investigated the Buddhist path and are convinced that taking refuge is the right step.

In the Theravada tradition, a lay person will formally request the Three Refuges from a monk, called a *bhikkhu* or a nun. To request the Three Refuges the lay person bows from the waist three times with the hands held together, as if in prayer, over the heart. The words are chanted in Pali. If taking refuge from a monk, as below, the word Bhante is used; if a nun, the word Ayye is substituted. For men requesting refuge the first of the two words separated by / is used, for women the second:

MAYAM/AHAM BHANTE TI-SARANENA SAHA PANCA SILANI YACAMA/YACAMI
*I, Venerable Sir, request the Three Refuges.*

DUTTYAMPI MAYAM/AHAM BHANTE TI-SARANENA SAHA PANCA SILANI YACAMA/YACAMI
*For the second time, Venerable Sir, I request the Three Refuges.*

TATIYAMPI MAYAM/AHAM BHANTE TI-SARANENA SAHA PANCA SILANI YACAMA/YACAMI
*For the third time, Venerable Sir, I request the Three Refuges.*

*The bikkhu recites the following three times, then the lay person recites them three times.*

NAMO TASSA BHAGAVATO ARAHATO SAMMASABUDDHASSA
*Homage to the Blessed One, the Noble One, and Perfectly Enlightened One.*

*The bhikkhu recites the following line by line, and the lay person repeats each line after him.*

BUDDHAM SARANAM GACCHAMI
*To the Buddha, I go for Refuge.*

DHAMMAM SARANAM GACCHAMI
*To the Dhamma, I go for Refuge.*

SANGHAM SARANAM GACCHAMI
*To the Sangha, I go for Refuge.*

*These three lines are repeated three times, prefixing* DUTTYAMPI *for the second time and* TATTYAMPI *for the third.*

*The bhikkhu says:*
TISARANA-GAMANAM NITTHITAM
*This completes the going for the Three Refuges.*

*The lay person replies:*
AMA BHANTE
*Yes, Venerable Sir.*

# zen chants to kuan shih yin

*To witness a full-scale performance of Kuan Yin's rites, it is best to visit a large temple, whether in China or Japan . . . during any of three great annual festivals . . .*

JOHN BLOFELD

Kuan Shih Yin is the great Zen Bodhisattva of compassion. *Bodhisattva* means "enlightenment being"—a fully enlightened being who chooses to remain in this world to help others rather than rest in nirvana. Her name means "she who listens to the cries of the world." Originally the Indian male Bodhisattva of compassion Avalokiteshvara, Kuan Yin gradually evolved into a goddess when Buddhism traveled to China. Kuan Yin retains a huge popular following in China and Japan, as well as in Korea and Vietnam.

In a traditional ceremony, an entire evening and night is spent in worship of Kuan Yin. The temple is cleaned scrupulously, and all participants take a ritual, purifying bath. A profusion of candles and incense burners is placed throughout the temple, and the altar is heaped with fruit and flowers. Zen Buddhist monks lead the ceremonies and chants, accompanied by rhythmic beating on fish-shaped wooden drums.

The following is one of the sonorous chants used to praise Kuan Yin that keeps the original male designation of the Bodhisattva. The rhythm of the chant is as important as the cryptic and elusive meaning of the words, typical of Zen.

*Kuan Shih Yin!*
*Hail Buddha!*
*In him, a cause!*
*In him, an outcome!*
*Buddha-Dharma-Sangha outcome!*
*Lasting joy, ego cleansed!*
*Morning, think Kuan Yin!*
*Evening, think Kuan Yin!*
*Each call from mind!*
*No call not mind-born!*

The highlight of the ceremony is the ritual invocation of Kuan Yin's name, repeated by the whole congregation time and again. Participants often feel touched by the compassionate presence of Kuan Yin at this point, and their devotion is heightened. The invocation below is meant to be chanted rhythmically many times. In traditional ceremonies, devotees also circumambulate the prominent statue of Kuan Yin during the chanting of her name.

NAMO KUAN SHIH YIN PÕU-SA!
*Hail to Kuan Shih Yin Bodhisattva!*

# tibetan mantra recitation using prayer beads

*Traditionally a Buddhist rosary, or* mala, *of 108 beads is used for mantra recitation.*

ROBERT BEER

There are many Tibetan Buddhist deities, such as Avalokiteshvara, who represents the Buddha's compassion, and Manjushri, who represents the Buddha's wisdom. Each deity has his or her own mantra that is a short phrase of sacred syllables, usually in ancient Sanskrit. Recitation of mantras is a devotional practice done either as part of a meditation session or integrated into daily life. Many Tibetans continuously recite mantras under their breath as they go about their daily business.

It is traditional to count each mantra using a string of prayer beads called a mala. Malas consist of either 108 or 21 beads threaded together on a string with a tassel joining the two ends. Mala beads can be made from various substances like sandalwood, moonstone, crystal, bone, and seeds. It is most effective to recite a complete cycle of 21 mantras each time. Daily recitation is recommended.

## Shakyamuni Buddha Mantra

• *Sit in the meditation posture with a Buddha statue in front of you, holding your mala in your right hand. Start at the beginning of the mala with the bead next to the tassel.*

• *Holding the first bead between your thumb and first finger, recite either aloud or under your breath:*
OM MUNI MUNI MAHA MUNAYE SOHA
*(pronounced om mooni mooni ma-ha moon-aye-ye so-ha).*

• *As you start the second recitation, move your thumb and first finger to the second bead, continuing until you reach the end bead.*

• *Dedicate any merit from reciting Buddha's mantra to the benefit of all beings.*

*Avalokiteshvara's mantra is* OM MANI PADME HUM *and the female deity Tara's mantra is* OM TARE TUTTARE TURE SOHA. *You can recite either of these mantras in addition to or instead of Shakyamuni Buddha's mantra. It is helpful to have a picture of Avalokiteshvara and Tara if you recite their mantras, but it is not essential because all deities are aspects of Buddha.*

# setting up an altar

*If you are so inclined, you can set up an altar nearby for pictures that inspire you, for example, or for candles, incense, or other offerings.*

KATHLEEN MCDONALD

Not all Buddhists have an altar and it is not an essential requirement of practicing Buddhism. But if the idea appeals to you, setting up an altar is a lovely way to cultivate and express devotion to the Buddha. However, if you do decide to set up an altar you must maintain it by keeping it clean and renewing the offerings every time you meditate; ideally this is a daily practice. Not maintaining the altar is disrespectful and of no spiritual benefit.

The different Buddhist traditions have different styles of altar, which are conditioned by culture as well as tradition. A typical Tibetan Buddhist altar has a colorful profusion of offerings, while a typical Zen altar might have only a simple statue of Buddha and an incense burner, or censer. One is not better than the other; each tradition has its own way of expressing devotion to the Buddha.

Traditional Buddhist objects, such as a Buddha statue, incense, and a *mala* (a twenty-one-bead string of prayer beads), offer an appropriate way for you to begin your devotional Buddhist practice. Later you may decide that you wish to practice according to one Buddhist tradition exclusively. At this stage you can choose a style of Buddha statue and type of incense that reflect your chosen Buddhist tradition.

Setting up an altar and making offerings on it creates an atmosphere conducive to meditation. The atmosphere can be enhanced by hanging a picture, poster, or picture card over the altar. This can be a representation of Buddha, one of the Buddhist deities, or a Buddhist teacher. When you begin devotional Buddhist practice it is more important to choose Buddhist images that appeal to you rather than being concerned about which tradition they represent.

Setting up your altar is simple. Choose a shelf or low side table in the room in which you meditate. You might like to cover it with an attractive cloth, but this is a personal choice and not essential. You can place a Buddha statue in the center, and put an incense burner and some prayer beads next to it. Descriptions of other objects that make suitable offerings, ways to make daily offerings, and instructions on how to make inner offerings to the Buddha are detailed on pages 120–121.

# making offerings

*The general purpose of offerings is to accumulate merit. Its particular function is to be the direct opponent to avarice.*

GESHE RABTEN

As described earlier, you can place a Buddha statue in the center of your altar. Everything you put around the statue now becomes an offering to the Buddha. You can make offerings every time before you meditate, and also do prostrations, described on pages 122–123.

To offer incense you will need to have an incense burner or holder. There are many varieties of incense holders designed for incense of different sizes. Before making your purchase, be sure that the aperture will fit your stick of incense. A simple alternative is to use a small bowl or Japanese teacup. Fill this with rice and, once lit, push the incense stick in a little way. The rice holds the incense firmly, and when it has burned down it simply goes out without burning the rice.

To actually offer incense, light it and let the flame go out so the fragrant smoke is released. Hold the incense stick between your hands in salutation posture and bow toward the Buddha. Then place the stick in the holder. The fragrant smoke contains traditional herbs and wood that have been used for centuries to help create a calm mood suitable for meditation.

Other traditional offerings include a small vase of carefully arranged flowers, a candle, and a water bowl. The point is to choose objects that are as beautiful and special as possible because you are offering them to the Buddha and to your own potential to awaken. There is no benefit in offering inferior objects. If you like, you can also place inspiring pictures or quotations on or near your altar.

When you place physical offerings on your altar you also make inner offerings. This means you remain mindful of why you are practicing meditation—to awaken—and you offer this pure intention to the Buddha. You can also make visualized offerings, which should be of the most beautiful, pure nature and as wonderful as you can imagine. In this way, even if you cannot afford to buy traditional incense or expensive flowers, you can still make offerings with devotion and gain spiritual merit.

# prostrations

*Prostration serves to purify negativities of the body, speech, and mind. In particular, it is the direct opponent of pride . . . It is important to overcome pride as it directly prevents the accumulation of merits.*

GESHE RABTEN

Performing prostrations is an act of devotion and respect, but it can seem to be a controversial practice for Westerners. If you are from a Christian or Jewish background, doing prostrations might appear to break one of the Ten Commandments, that of bowing down to graven images. However, when we prostrate in front of a statue of the Buddha, the real objects we are paying reverence to are the Buddha's enlightened qualities and our own potential to awaken. In this way, we are not mindlessly prostrating to an image but are performing an authentic devotional Buddhist practice.

It is customary to prostrate in front of the altar whenever you enter a shrine room in a Buddhist temple or monastery. Prostrations are done three times, once to each of the Three Objects of Refuge: the Buddha; his teachings, the Dharma; and the spiritual community, the Sangha. When we prostrate physically with our body, we also prostrate with our speech by silently reciting a prayer praising the Buddha, Dharma, and Sangha, as well as with our mind by cultivating devotional respect and faith in the Three Refuges.

## How to Prostrate

Each tradition has its own form of prostration or bowing. Described below is the Tibetan Buddhist way of prostrating. As you prostrate, be mindful that you are prostrating to the Buddha's enlightened qualities and your potential to awaken—what the statue represents rather than its material being. You can prostrate in front of your altar three times before you start meditating, with deep respect and as a reminder that you are actively nurturing your buddha nature.

- *Start by standing upright, feet shoulder-width apart.*
- *Raise your hands above your head, palms together in salutation.*
- *Move your hands in turn to your forehead, throat, and heart.*
- *Fall to your hands and knees and touch your forehead to the floor.*
- *Stand up and repeat twice more so you have completed three prostrations.*

# healing through devotion to Tara

*I am a teacher, and, like a doctor, I can give you effective medicine, but you have to take it yourself and look after yourself.*

THE BUDDHA

One of the most beloved deities in Tibetan Buddhism is White Tara. Tara's special gift is her ability to heal devotees of physical and emotional ills. Visualizing Tara and chanting her mantra has brought healing and peace of mind to many people.

You can use the following visualization to reach out to Tara for healing.

• *Study a picture of White Tara (see page 24 for example). Close your eyes and bring to your mind's eye an image of Tara sitting before you. Include as much detail as you can. Tell yourself that your visualized Tara is not simply a "picture" but an actual living representation of the Buddha's compassion, like a loving mother who is ready and willing to help you.*

• *Make a strong request to Tara to heal any physical ailments you have. Tara responds by sending out light from her heart that gathers physical healing in the form of golden-yellow light. This light returns to Tara and flows from her into you, washing you inside and out, relieving your physical symptoms and illnesses.*

• *Now ask Tara to heal your emotional problems, such as anxiety, fear, jealousy, and other negative states of mind. In answer, Tara sends out light from her heart and gathers emotional healing in the form of milky-white light. This light returns to Tara and flows from her into you, alleviating your emotional problems.*

• *Next ask Tara to balance your body's energies, giving you the "heat" you need to digest food and heal any problems you have with low energy and lack of vitality or with fiery or impulsive tendencies. Tara gathers the power to balance your energies in the form of ruby-red light. The light flows from her into you, balancing your body's energies.*

• *Now ask Tara to heal any problems with your mind, such as difficulty concentrating, memory problems, or mental dullness. Tara sends out light to gather healing in the form of emerald-green light, which she pours into you, soothing your mind.*

• *Ask Tara to heal the "space" within your body-mind. Too much space can make you feel out-of-touch. Too little can make you feel oppressed. Tara gathers healing energy in the form of sapphire-blue light that flows into you, giving you room to move, grow, and develop spiritually.*

• *The power of this healing exercise is increased if you chant or recite Tara's mantra as you visualize:* OM TARE TUTTARE TURE SOHA *(pronounced om ta-ray too-ta-ray too-ray so-ha). Say the mantra as many times as you can as you do the steps of the visualization above.*

# index

A
advice 50–1
altars 118–20, 122–4
Amitabha 98–9
attitudes 85
auspicious days 108–9

B
benefits 44–5
Bodhidharma 83–4
Bodhisattva 72, 114

C
China 72–3, 83–4, 91, 98, 109, 114
compassion 24–5
concentration 30–1
contentment 12–13

D
daily life 66–7
Dalai Lama 44, 91
death 32–3
devotional practices 7, 64, 99, 102–25
Dharma 10, 20–1, 112, 115, 122

E
Eightfold Path 19, 36–9

F
faith 104–5
festivals 108–9, 110–11
Friends of the Western Buddhist
Order 100

G
generosity 26–7, 39

H
Healing 124-5
Higher Trainings 36

I
impermanence 11, 31–3, 44
incense 7, 119, 120–1
India 6, 70–4, 92
Indra's Jeweled Net 34–5
informal practice 66–7, 99
insight 58–61, 76, 93
interdependence 34–5

J
Japan 73, 83–4, 98, 114
Jewels 20–1, 23
joyful effort 28–9

K
koans 82–7
Korea 73, 83, 114
Kuan Shih Yin 114–15

L
lamas 92–3
life story 14–15
love 24–5, 65
lovingkindness 34–5, 78–9

M
Mahayana 71–3, 92
malas 116, 119
mandalas 64, 90, 93
mantras 99, 111, 116–17, 125

meditation 40–67, 78–81, 86–9, 94–7
mindfulness 54–8, 65–7, 80–1, 95–7
monastics 75–6, 83, 90–3, 107–8
morality 26–7, 36

N

Nichiren 73, 99
nirvana 19–20, 110
Noble Truths 18–19, 36

O

offerings 119–21

P

patience 28–9
Poisons 22–3
prayer beads 7, 116–17, 119
preparation 48–9
principles 7, 8–39
problem-solving 52–3
prostrations 109, 111, 120, 122–3
Pure Land 73, 98–9

R

rebirth 94–5
refuge prayer 21, 112–13
Refuges 112–13, 122
relevance 16–17
Rinzai 73, 84–5

S

Sangha 21, 112, 115, 122
sensations 80–1
Shakyamuni 11–12, 15, 117
Shuddhodana 14
Siddhartha 14–16
sitting position 46–7
Soto 73, 84–5, 88
Sri Lanka 71, 74, 76, 110
statue 7, 30, 49, 105, 119, 120, 122–3
stress 12–13, 45, 51, 59
Sutras 70, 74, 80, 93

T

Tantra 93
Tara 124-5
teachers 93, 106–7, 108, 112, 119
Thailand 71, 74, 76, 110
Theravada 71–2, 74–7, 80, 83, 108, 111–13, 119
Tibet 73, 83, 90–3, 109–11, 116–19, 123
traditions 7, 68–101, 107–8, 110, 119, 121

V

vipassana 76
visualization 64–5

W

walking 53, 62–3, 67
Wesak 110–11
Wheel of Life 22–3
wisdom 15, 20, 27, 30–1, 36, 39, 44, 59, 65

Z

Zazen 88–9
Zen 72–3, 82–5, 92, 109, 111, 114–15, 119

# acknowledgments

Designed and produced for Godsfield Press
by The Bridgewater Book Company

*Project Designer* Anna Hunter-Downing
*Project Editor* Nicola Wright
*Picture Researcher* Vanessa Fletcher

*Picture credits*
ROBERT BEER: pp. 24, 49, 78; CORBIS: Cover inset David Samuel Robbins, pp. 8/9 Luca I. Tettoni, 21 Paul W. Liebhardt, 28 Jon Feingersh, 31 Earl & Nazima Kowall, 44 Chris Lisle, 51 Brian Leng, 68/69 Chris Lisle, 104 Jeremy Horner, 110 Tom Nebbia, 113 Tiziana & Gianni Baldizzone; THE HUTCHISON LIBRARY: pp.11 Michael Macintyre, 29 Vanessa S. Boeye, 40/41 Patricio Goycoolea, 74 Nigel Smith, 80 Nigel Howard, 84 Patricio Goycoolea, 90 Carlos Friere, 92 & 100 Nigel Howard, 107 Patricio Goycoolea, 109 John Burbank, 118 Nigel Howard